YOUTHS SERVING YOUTHS IN DRUG EDUCATION PROGRAMS

George R. Taylor

ScarecrowEducation
Lanham, Maryland • Toronto • Oxford
2004

362.2917
T241y
2004

Published in the United States of America
by ScarecrowEducation
An imprint of The Rowman & Littlefield Publishing Group, Inc.
4501 Forbes Boulevard, Suite 200, Lanham, Maryland 20706
www.scarecroweducation.com

PO Box 317
Oxford
OX2 9RU, UK

British Library Cataloguing in Publication Information Available

Library of Congress Cataloging-in-Publication Data
Taylor, George R.
  Youths serving youths in drug education programs / George R. Taylor.
      p. cm.
  Includes bibliographical references and index.
  ISBN 1-57886-039-3 (pbk. : alk. paper)
  1. Youth–Drug use–United States–Prevention. 2. Drug abuse–United
States–Prevention. 3. Drug abuse–Study and teaching–United States.
I. Title.
HV5824.Y68 T39 2004
362.29'17'08340973–dc22   2003017044

∞[TM] The paper used in this publication meets the minimum requirements of
American National Standard for Information Sciences—Permanence of
Paper for Printed Library Materials, ANSI/NISO Z39.48-1992.
Manufactured in the United States of America.

This textbook is dedicated to all the learners who have attended and are attending my drug seminars conducted at the Union Institute and University, and to the personnel in the public and private sectors serving youths with addictive behaviors. Many of the concepts advanced in this text can be attributed to their devotion and insight.

CONTENTS

ACKNOWLEDGMENTS

This textbook is written for all personnel involved in treating youths with drug abuse problems in all segment of our society. The text is premised upon the fact that early intervention, treatment, and evaluation are key components in reducing drug abuse.

The final revision of this textbook could not have been completed without the assistance of the editorial staff at ScarecrowEducation Press, Dr. Marcella Brooks, and Dr. Patrick O'Reilly for reviewing and correcting the manuscript. A special thank you is in order to Emma "Sisie" Crosby for her commitment and dedication in typing and retyping numerous drafts of the manuscript.

PREFACE

Strategies advanced in this textbook were designed to reduce, eradicate, or minimize the use of drugs among youths in this country. One key concept is prevention, based upon the developmental stage of individuals and on total involvement from the schools, community, parents, and the media, with respect to the cultural values found therein. In order to achieve this, I recommend an approach called *Youths Serving Youths in Drug Education Programs (Y.S.Y.D.E.)*. Chapters are designed to apprise educators on how Y.S.Y.D.E. can be applied to reduce drug usage among youths.

❶

DRUG PREVENTION INTERVENTION

Recent statistics show that most high school seniors nationwide have used an illicit drug at least once and that 40 percent of them have used cocaine by the time they are seventeen (Temple and Fillmore 1986; National Institute on Drug Abuse 1997; U.S. Department of Health and Human Services 1998; National Clearinghouse for Alcohol and Drug Information 1997). Investigators at the University of Michigan reported that 17 percent of 1985 college students had used cocaine in the previous month (Johnston, O'Malley, and Bachman 1998). Data also reflects that most youth who use drugs have become addicted to them. According to Kandel (1984) and Oetting and Beauvais (1988), most youth involvement with drugs is strongly associated with peer-group membership. One major conclusion that can be drawn is that developing comprehensive prevention programs may save many of our youth from becoming addicts.

When the age range is moved back to between nine and twelve, most children in this age range have not become addicted to drugs because of early drug intervention programs in the elementary grades. This is a crucial age to expand drug and alcohol preventive programs in schools. Alcohol, in contrast to popular belief, is a drug. Research conducted by Flatter and McCormick (1989) claimed that 20 percent of our children have experimented with alcohol or other drugs by the seventh grade. Reasons for experimenting with drugs are varied and complex; however, using an interdisciplinary approach to confront the drug problems in infancy—starting when youths are in prekindergarten (ages three to five)—causes drug abuse by youths ages nine to twelve to substantially decline (Segal and Steward 1996; Ayers 1989; Butler 1989; Dewit 1994; Hahn, Hall, Rayens, Burt, Corley, and Sheffel 2000).

A first step in developing a comprehensive drug program is to assess the community's needs. These crucial issues are addressed in detail in chapter 7. Because developing drug programs can be expensive for many school districts, section 4116 of the Improving America's Schools Act of 1994, Local Drug and Violence/Prevention Programs, provides funds to aid local educational agencies in developing comprehensive drug educational programs. Refer to appendix A for specific details on this program.

A second priority is for the schools to develop in-service workshops for educators, by using funds from section 4116. These workshops should be conducted by competent specialists to cover the wide spectrum of illegal, legal, moral, social, educational, physical, medical, and psychological factors inherent with drug abuse. Part of the training for educators should involve ways to be nonjudgmental and honest, as well as ways to develop a genuine concern for the student. Training should also stress the importance of peer relationships on drug usage. Peer groups are frequently more important than the pressures of the school and home environments. It is virtually impossible for youths to refrain from using drugs at the same time their intimate peers are using them. Specific strategies and interventions must focus on the causes and treatments of drug abuse (King, Wagner, and Hedrick 2001).

A third priority is to develop a conceptual framework for conducting the program. Recommended conceptual frameworks for a drug prevention program are based upon Bandura's social learning theory (1977, 1986). This theory assumes that individuals are neither determined entirely by internal causes nor solely by the result of environmental constraints. Further, the theory claims that internal factors have a central role in determining behavior but that new responses may be learned by observations or changed through cognitive processes. The intervention strategies developed in chapter 5 are based upon youths seeing good models who demonstrate how to bring all behaviors involving drugs to the conscious level before reacting. Before drug abuse can be brought to the conscious levels of youths, educators must understand the many factors associated with drug abuse.

WHY CHILDREN USE DRUGS

Children use drugs for many reasons; their behaviors have been warped by enormous social pressures, especially in an environment of unmet need. It is most likely that a child's temptation to use drugs will occur in a social situation with his or her peers. Peer pressure becomes a major influence on our children during their elementary years. Children begin having desires for certain clothes and friends, and are tempted to experiment with drugs. Some experts believe that the peer pressure argument is a cop-out for doing things that youths know are wrong. Others believe that peer pressure is dominant because of a lack of parenting skills and parental involvement in our society. Whatever the reasons, children are faced with this issue of peer pressure in elementary schools and the problem continues through high school, where drug abuse rapidly increases. Because children use peer pressure to make decisions, it is one of the many problems involving their association with drugs. Peer pressure regarding drug use and abuse will continue to influence our children's minds as long as our youths find positive reinforcement for drug use from our society (Dobson 1990, 1).

Children are affected in many different ways by drugs in their environments, whether or not they use drugs themselves. In some cases, it could be a parent who is addicted. Children who experience this lifestyle tend to live with loneliness, confusion, lack of parental guidance, lack of love, and low self-esteem. These children tend to become addicts, commit suicide, or become role models (both positive and negative) for others. If a child chooses to make a stand, he or she is generally either very successful throughout life or blames others for his or her failures. Other causes of drug abuse involve siblings who use drugs, which in turn affects the whole family. Families begin to fall apart and attitudes change between parent and child, even a child who is not yet using drugs. Children may isolate themselves from family involvement and begin to manipulate parents. During this time, drugs have made either a negative or positive influence on the brother or sister, and such effects can last a lifetime. Memories of that time will stay with the child forever and will influence decisions made later in life.

Children raised in poverty often suffer from debilitating deprivations that may be responsible for drugs, violence, apathy, low expectations, poor self-images, racism, and classism, and that have a significant impact on their self-esteem. This is especially true for children with disabilities (Taylor 1997).

One of the most difficult tasks educators face is preventing individuals with disabilities from becoming substance abusers (Cardoso, Desilva, Thomas, Roldan, and Ingraham 1966). The disability may cover up any substance abuse used by the student. Educators must become acutely aware of the possibility of this condition. In the case where a student with a disability has a substance abuse problem, the educator must address both issues. It is hoped that initial intervention strategies will eliminate the need for substance abuse treatment.

Individuals with disabilities vary significantly in the types of intervention needed. Factors such as the type of psychosocial problems, availability of support systems within the schools, levels of motivation, and interpersonal relationships need to be comprehensively assessed. Educators may need to refer students to specialists, depending upon the needs assessed, if they are not competent in the assessed areas (Nineteenth Annual Report to Congress on the Implementation of Individual with Disabilities Education Act 1997) Referrals may have to be made for students (1) who have severe types of disabilities, (2) who have experimented with drugs, and (3) whose histories cannot distinguish whether the disability or the substance abuse is the reason for the unacceptable behavior. Many drug prevention strategies have to be adapted and modified to meet the unique needs of individuals with disabilities. Regardless of the status or classification of youths using drugs, individual intervention strategies should be developed to eliminate or reduce drug usage. During my years of experience, I elected to use psychosocial interventions because the schools are better equipped to use these interventions when compared with other models of intervention.

PSYCHOSOCIAL INTERVENTIONS

Causes of drug abuse vary from community to community, based upon the unique characteristics of each. Once the causes have been identified, intervention programs should be developed to reduce the risks of substance abuse among youth (Schinke, Botvin, and Orlandi 1991; Greenwood 1992; Botvin 1986; Cahalan 1991). These programs should be interdisciplinary in order to meet the many physical, psychological, and social problems inherent in drug abuse.

Specialists in various fields should be invited to support the intervention program. Specialists should schedule visits to the schools at regular intervals, depending upon the age and interest of the group. Some of the specialists involved in the intervention may include physicians, pharmacists, lawyers, clergymen, psychologists, social workers, mental health specialists, and any other local, state, or federal departments deemed necessary to successfully complete the intervention (Segal and Steward 1996; Schinke, Botvin, and Orlandi 1991; Goldstein 1993). A detailed description of behavioral intervention is found in chapter 5. Several types of drug intervention models are in the psychosocial area. The most widely used one is Drug Abuse Resistance Education (D.A.R.E.).

DRUG ABUSE RESISTANCE EDUCATION

Drug Abuse Resistance Education (D.A.R.E.) is the most popular drug education program in the country. Approximately 70 percent of schools in the country as well as forty-four foreign countries have adapted the program. Recently, however, the effectiveness of the program has been under attack. Data suggest that the program has not significantly reduced substance abuse among youth in this country (*Law Enforcement News* 1996; Clayton, Cattarello, and Johnstone 1996).

According to Botvin, Baker, and others (1990), the program is based upon social skills and a social influence model of drug education. Students engage in role-playing and other social activities to resist peer offers of drug use. Many strategies in the program are based upon a psychosocial approach (refer to chapter 2 for special details). D.A.R.E. is designed to prevent children in kindergarten through grade 12 from using drugs. School and community agencies collaborate on the activities, which involve the use of competent police officers to teach drug prevention in the schools. The program was created in 1983 as a collaborative agreement between the Los

Angeles Police Department and the Los Angeles United School District, and has grown to be the largest drug education program in the world (Botvin, Baker, et al. 1990; California State Department of Education 1968 Clayton, Cattarello, Day, and Walden 1991; Hansen 1989).

The psychosocial intervention models discussed in chapters 2, 5, and 7 have been adapted from the D.A.R.E. model. It is believed that this intervention strategy can be effectively administered in the schools with minimum training for school and community personnel and, like all intervention strategies, is designed to eradicate or reduce drug abuse.

INTERVENTION STRATEGIES

Intervention strategies should be designed to stop the substance abuse before it begins. They should be carefully planned with appropriate resources and personnel. Sessions should not be mandatory; students should have the option of attending. Some type of schedule should be developed and adhered to throughout the sessions. As much as possible, students should be involved in planning strategies that are varied and based on community needs (Schinke, Botvin, and Orlandi 1991; Brown 1997; Winters 1990).

DEVELOPMENT OF STRATEGIES

Some basic intervention strategies should be in place to assist administrators in developing intervention strategies. Several strategies have been developed; guidelines for evaluating strategies are listed. These strategies are not exhaustive, as there are many approaches in developing functional and realistic programs. Intervention strategies should:

1. *Target all forms of drug abuse.* Students should know that many forms of substances have potential abuse, including salt, sugar, aspirin, and most medicines. Others include overuse of tobacco, coffee, alcohol, inhalants, and chemical-dependent drugs, if not taken under controlled conditions (Goode 1993; Cohen 1996).

2. *Be designed to reverse or reduce known risk factors that may promote the use of drugs.* Common risk factors are alluded to earlier in the chapter. Many are culturally, socially, and psychologically based. These risk factors must be identified and intervention strategies developed to minimize them (Elias et al. 1997; Davis, Wolfe, Orenstein, Bergamo, Buetens, Fraster, Hogan, MacLean, and Ryan 1994). These strategies may involve integration and collaboration with various local, state, and federal agencies.

3. *Include skills to refuse drugs when offered by introducing ways to reinforce attitudes against drug use.* Some activities may include improving the social competency of students through communication, peer relations, self-efficacy, decision making, problem solving, and stress reduction. Students must be taught how to be assertive by using role-playing; creating dramas, videos, filmstrips, and films; modeling techniques; and participating in peer group and individual discussions (Harding, Safer, Kavanagh, Bania, Carty, Lisnov, and Wysockey 1996; Brown and Stetson 1988).

4. *Include a parent component that is designed to reinforce intervention strategies taught in school.* Parents should receive in-service training that includes facts about the harmful effects of drugs, identification of legal and illegal drugs, and strict family policies against drug usage. Additionally, the training should give parents ways of making intervention strategies a family problem (Peele 1996; Kay and Cohen 1998; Kelker 1990; Catalano, Kosterman, Haggerty, Hawkins, and Spoth 1998).

5. *Develop long-term and community-wide policies from kindergarten through the senior high school level, infusing and integrating the material within the normal curricula to assist in transition from one level to another* (Winters 1990; Perry 1986; Botvin 1991).

6. *Include media announcements on policy changes in substance abuse and the harmful effects of using drugs.* Examples include legislation that restricts youth from purchasing alcohol or tobacco products. This process becomes effective with widespread support from families, schools, churches, and the community (Kaplin 1996).

7. *Be adapted to reflect the specific nature of the drug problem in the local community.* An assessment of community needs should be

undertaken to determine the nature and extent of the drug problem in each community (Johnson 1986). Several types of instruments may be developed, including questionnaires, surveys, rating scales, observational scales, checklists, and interviews to assess student, parent, and community views toward the drug problem in the community. The school district's research and evaluation office is a recommended place to construct, administer, and evaluate the instrument. It should also be responsible for assigning priorities for addressing the drug problem (St. Pierre, Kaltreider, et al. 1992; Pentz 1986).

8. *Consider the risk factors that can cause youths to convert to substance abuse.* Many risk factors can contribute to increased substance abuse. They have been categorized into five broad categories (Hawkins and Catalano 1992).

   a. Individual and interpersonal risk factors: low self-esteem, genetic susceptibility, sensation seeking, antisocial behavior, aggressiveness, early first use of drugs, conduct problems, favorable attitudes toward drugs, shyness, rebelliousness, friends who use drugs, alienation, academic failure, low commitment to school, and so on.

   b. Peer group factors: associating with individuals who use illegal drugs, rejection in elementary grades, friendship with other rejected children, bonding with peers who abuse alcohol and drugs and engage in other delinquent activities, peer pressure to use substances, and association with peers who abuse substances. Associating with substance-abusing peers is the final determinant of substance abuse among many youth. Peer influences involve changing behaviors to meet expectations of others (Burns and Darling 2002). Resistance to peer pressure can be increased through involvement in peer resistance training programs.

   c. Family risk factors: alcoholic parents; family history of alcoholism; perceived parent permissiveness toward drug/alcohol use; family management problems; lack of or inconsistent parental discipline; negative communication patterns; conflict; low bonding; stress and dysfunction caused by death, divorce, incarceration of parents; low income; lack of skills to cope with family problems; parental rejection (for example, the unwanted child); lack of adult supervision; lack of family ritual (such as holiday family gatherings); poor family management and communication; physical or sexual abuse; and parental or sibling substance abuse. Strengthening families can reduce the negative effects of family environmental influences on youth for substance abuse. Prevention strategies can include conducting parenting programs, providing family support, and providing family skills training. Family therapy has been found to reduce the effects of substance abuse risk factors, including delinquency, misconduct, and depression.

d. School risk factors: lack of support for positive school values and attitudes, early antisocial behavior, school dysfunction, high rates of substance abuse and pro-substance abuse norms, drug-using gang members, low teacher and student morale, school climate that provides little encouragement and support, student perceptions that teachers do not care about them, lack of appreciation for school and educational process, academic failure, lack of involvement in school due to discrimination, lack of opportunities for involvement and reward, perceived unfair rules, and norms that are conducive to substance abuse. School climate improvement programs have been effective in reducing the negative effects of adolescent substance abuse.

e. Community risk factors: high crime rate, high population density, community norms favoring drug usage, physical deterioration, norms supporting alcohol and other drug abuse, ambivalent or pro-substance abuse community values and attitudes, community dysfunction, transient populations, lack of active community institutions, lack of inclusion in the community, being in a community that condones substance abuse, disorganized neighborhoods lacking leadership, lack of opportunities for youth involvement in positive activities, high rates of substance abuse, poverty and lack of employment opportunities, easy availability of drugs and alcohol, and lack of economic mobility and social supports. Increased opportunities for positive community involvement may reduce the effects of the negative environmental influences on youth for substance abuse.

Survey research studies often are used also as the basis for identifying risk factors based on demographic factors. Demographic factors include gender, ethnicity, age, socioeconomic status, employment, income, education, and location of residency. Other psychological approaches include cognitive behavior intervention strategies that can be successfully conducted by educators.

COGNITIVE BEHAVIOR INTERVENTION

Several studies have attested to the values of using cognitive behavioral intervention to deter and prevent drug abuse among youth (Botvin, Baker, et al. 1990; Webb 1993). One study exposed subjects to five treatment conditions: (1) a prevention program without teaching life skills led by older students, (2) a prevention program with life skills and booster sessions taught by older students, (3) a teacher-led prevention program without life skills, (4) a teacher-led program with life skills and booster sessions, and (5) a test-retest control group. The sample included 1,185 eighth-grade students. Students and teachers involved in the experimental study were trained in the use of a booster prevention program that involved intervention strategies and activities like basic life skills to improve coping mechanisms to resist substance abuse. The control group was not exposed to the experimental conditions. Findings of the study revealed that older student leaders produced significantly fewer users of alcohol, tobacco, and marijuana (Webb 1993).

The lack of students admitting to the use of drugs may be attributed to the lack of urban students included in the study, and to teachers who did not support the experimental program. However, other studies might yield significant differences between the two group groups using the experimental conditions if they were to eliminate the pitfalls of the study. Modifications and accommodations would have to be made for instructing individuals with disabilities.

INSTRUCTING THE DISABLED IN DRUG ABUSE

As an educator responsible for the education of children with disabilities, there is a need to be sensitive to family issues. Many families of individuals with disabilities have had negative experiences with social agencies and may not trust the school's intervention plan. This may lead some educators to conclude that the family has little interest in the intervention plan. Attempts should be made to appreciate the fact that many families with disabled individuals are resourceful in dealing with the problems of having a disabled child, and isolated events as stated will not apply to all families.

Some recommended strategies that educators can employ when developing and implementing an intervention plan are:

1. Assess the strengths and weaknesses of the family to assist with the intervention plan.
2. Validate the cause, if possible, of the disability through checking official documents and school records.
3. Suggest responsibilities that family members should take in implementing the plan.
4. Outline specific strategies that each family member can assume in carrying out the plan.
5. Initiate strategies to manage the emotional and financial burden imposed on the family because of the disability.
6. Inform parents of the many community resources, self-help groups, vocational training, and sources of financial assistance available.
7. Be prepared to recommend students for services outside the school, if the school does not have the expertise to serve the student.
8. Realize that disability in the family creates undue hardships. When combined with substance abuse, the problem is magnified. The degree of magnification depends upon the degree of disability, the length of time the disability has been present, and the reactions of peers and other family members to the disability. An individual with a disability and a substance abuse problem can significantly affect all family functioning, including the atmosphere, assumed roles, rules, relationships, and the ability to solve problems (Heineman 1993).

This list illustrates the importance of early intervention to reduce or minimize the number of individuals with disabilities resorting to substance abuse. Additionally, an individual with a disability and a substance abuse problem can deplete the family financial resources and set up a state of hopelessness for the entire family. Implementation of these strategies should reduce the financial burdens on families.

When planning drug prevention programs, the following guidelines are highly recommended for consideration in order to produce effective programs and to avoid the low success rates evident in many drug programs (Greenwood 1992; Davis, Wolfe, et al. 1994; Centers for Disease Control and Prevention 1998; Newcomb 1995). Effective program recommendations include:

1. Begin early, if it is to be effective. Children as early as kindergartners should be educated about drugs and their harmful effects (White and Pitts 1998; Kaplin 1996). The danger of taking medications found in the home may be a place to start. Specific strategies for teaching this group are delineated in chapter 8.
2. Prepare professional training and competent school and community personnel in preventive strategies (Glen 1994; Fisher and Harrison 1993; Elmquist 1990; Flood and Morehouse 1986).
3. Be culturally sensitive. Cultural differences must be addressed when developing drug intervention strategies. The uniqueness of cultural styles differs from culture to culture. Children born into poverty and neglect often suffer from debilitating deprivations that may seriously impair their ability to learn and their self-esteem. Children are a product of their environments and tend to imitate experiences to which they are exposed. Many have seen poor models who frequently encourage the use of drugs. Out of the respect for cultural differences, educators must be flexible in developing intervention strategies (Grob and DeRios 1992; Johnson et al. 1990; Botvin, Schinke, and Orlandi 1995).
4. Find as many ways as possible for youths to take responsibility for making decisions relevant to drug education and curriculum development.
5. Find ways for youths to apply the crucial thinking skills that are essential to drug education. Youths need to be permitted to gather information from many sources relevant to drug abuse and education, reflect on them, and then make decisions.

SUMMARY

School systems throughout the country are seeking innovative strategies to prevent substance abuse among students. The literature is filled with research evaluating the drug problem, but few of these programs appear successful in preventing drug abuse (U.S. General Accounting Office 1990, 1993). Unfortunately, many youths are using drugs; 61 percent of students in U.S. high schools say drugs are used, kept, or sold in their schools. Adults and young people themselves must continue to try to find the answer to what works in stopping kids from using drugs, including alcohol and tobacco. Surveys from young people in Kansas City revealed that they want more parental involvement in their lives. This is a clear place to start in searching for antidrug programs that work. Schools need the support and encouragement of parents in their efforts to prevent usage. PTAs can play a valuable role in keeping parents informed through monthly and annual meetings, where the school's approach to drug education can be explained. This may assist parents in overcoming any initial alarm at the prospect of their children being taught about drugs and concern that such teaching may encourage experimentation. At these meetings, parents can observe teaching materials to be used and meet outside professionals, such as police officers or health professionals, and ascertain the specific roles they will play in the program. This is an excellent opportunity for the school to directly involve parents in the program. This collaboration can demonstrate to parents that the school is committed to educating all children about the harmful effects of drugs, and reinforce the knowledge that they cannot achieve this goal alone.

The construction and implementation of a drug prevention program is a complex endeavor. It should involve all stakeholders, reflect the characteristics of the target population, and take into account the risk factors that may contribute to drug usage (Swan 1995; U.S. Department of Health and Human Services 1993, 1998; National Clearinghouse for Alcohol and Drug Information 1997). Data in chapters 6 and 7 attest to this fact. It is the opinion of Botvin (1986, 1991) and White and Pitt (1998) that reduction in substance abuse must start with comprehensive prevention programs, such as social skills training and life-skills training models.

Effective substance abuse programs operating in schools should include the individual characteristics, culture, and risk factors (discussed earlier in this chapter) of the targeted populations' patterns of substance abuse. These factors must be understood and reflected in any substance prevention program (Kumpfer 1992; National Clearinghouse for Alcohol and Drug Information 1997; Fisher, Storck, and Bacon 1999).

Because multiple factors are associated with substance abuse, a primary preventive strategy would be to reduce or eliminate the risk factors associated with promoting substance abuse. The psychosocial approach advanced by Bandura (1977, 1986) appears to be a time-proven approach to reducing substance abuse among youth.

There are several types of intervention programs, such as legal and medical. I have chosen to use psychosocial intervention models because they appear to be more amenable for educators to implement in the schools. This view should not diminish the importance of legal and medical interventions. In many instances, they may be the best to use. Again, this chapter is designed to indicate how intervention strategies can prevent youths from turning to drugs. The schools have a monopoly on youths; using the strategies outlined in this chapter can significantly reduce the number of future drug addicts.

REFERENCES

Ayers, W. 1989. Childhood at risk. *Educational Leadership* 46, no. 8:70–72.

Bandura, A. 1977. *Social learning theory*. Englewood Cliffs, N.J.: Prentice Hall.

———. 1986. *Social foundations of thought and action: A social cognitive theory*. Englewood Cliffs, N.J.: Prentice Hall.

Botvin, G. J. 1986. Substance abuse prevention research: Recent developments and future directions. *Journal of School Health* 56, no. 9:369–74.

———. 1991. *Tobacco, alcohol, and drug abuse prevention through life skills training: Generalizability to multiple populations*. Ithaca, N.Y.: Cornell Medical College, Department of Public Health.

Botvin, G. J., E. F. Baker, et al. 1990. A cognitive-behavioral approach to substance abuse prevention: One-year follow-up. *Addict Behavior* 15:47–63.

Botvin, G. J., S. O. Schinke, and M. A. Orlandi. 1995. *Drug abuse prevention with multiethnic youth*. Thousand Oaks, Calif.: Sage Publications.

Brown, J. H. 1997. Listen to the kids. *American School Board Journal* 184:38–47.

Brown, S. A., and N. A. Stetson. 1988. Coping with drinking pressures: Adolescent parent perspectives. *Adolescence* 23:297–301.

Burns, A., and N. Darling. 2002. Peer influence or peer pressure? *Education Digest* 68, no. 2:4–6.

Bulter, O. B. 1989. Early help for kids at risk: Our nation's best investment. *NEA Today* 7, no. 6:56–58.

Cahalan, D. 1991. *An ounce of prevention: Strategies for solving tobacco, alcohol, and drug problems*. San Francisco, Calif.: Jossey-Bass.

California State Department of Education. 1968. *A study of more effective education relative to narcotics, other harmful drugs, and hallucinogenic substances. A progress report submitted to the California Legislative as required by Chapter 1437, Statutes of 1968*. Sacramento: California State Department of Education.

Cardoso, E., C. F. Desilva, K. R. Thomas, G. Roldan, and K. Ingraham. 1966. *Substance abuse and disability: The Hatherleigh guide to treating substance abuse*. Part 2. New York: Hatherleigh Press.

Catalano, R. F., R. Kosterman, K. Haggerty, J. Hawkins, and R. Spoth. 1998. A universal intervention for prevention of substance abuse: Preparing for the drug years. In *Drug abuse prevention through family intervention*, edited by R. Ashery, E. Robertson, and K. Kumpfer, 130–59. Washington, D.C.: U. S. Department of Health and Human Services. NIH Publication No. 97-4135.

Centers for Disease Control and Prevention. 1998. Youth risk behavior surveillance: United States, 1997, at www.cdc.gov/ncdcphp/dash/yrbs (accessed October 1, 2003).

Clayton, R. R., A. Cattarello, L. E. Day, and I. C. P. Walden. 1991. Persuasive communication and drug prevention: An evaluation of the DARE Program. In *Persuasive communication and drug abuse prevention*, edited by L. Donoher, H. Syper, and W. Bukoski. Hillsdale, N.J.: Lawrence Erlbaum.

Clayton, R. R., A. M. Cattarello, and B. M. Johnstone. 1996. The effectiveness of drug abuse resistance education (Project DARE): Five-year follow-up results. *Preventive Medicine* 25:307–18.

Cohen, J. 1996. Drug education: Politics, propaganda, and censorship. *International Journal of Drug Policy* 7, no. 3:153–57.

Davis, R. B., H. Wolfe, A. Orenstein, P. Bergamo, K. Buetens, B. Fraster, J. Hogan, A. MacLean, and M. Ryan. 1994. Intervening with high-risk youth: A program model. *Adolescence* 29:763–74.

Dewit, P. E. 1994. The crucial early years. *Time Magazine*, no. 143:16, 68.

Dobson, J., and G. Bauer. 1990. *Children at risk: The battle for the hearts and minds of our kids*. Dallas, Tex.: Word Publishing.

Elias, M. et al. 1997. *Promoting social and emotional learning: Guidelines for educators*. Alexandria, Va.: Association for Supervision and Curriculum Development.

Elmquist, D. L. 1990. School-based alcohol and other drug prevention programs: Guidelines for the special educator. *Intervention in School and Clinic* 27, no. 1:10–19.

Fisher, G. L., and T. C. Harrison. 1993. The school counselor's role in relapse prevention. *School Counselor* 41:120–25.

Fisher, P. A., M. Storck, and J. G. Bacon. 1999. In the eye of the beholder: Risk and protective factors in rural American Indian and Caucasian adolescents. *American Journal of Orthopsychiatry* 69, no. 3:294–304.

Flatter, C., and K. C. McCormick. 1989. *Learning to live drug free*. Alexandria, Va.: U.S. National School Board Association.

Flood, D. H., and E. R. Morehouse. 1986. The principal's role in preventing and reducing student substance abuse. *NASSP Bulletin* 70, no. 487:10–15.

Glen, M. K. 1994. Preparing rehabilitation specialists to address the prevention of substance abuse problems. *Rehabilitation Counseling Bulletin* 38:164–79.

Goldstein, E. G. 1993. The borderline abuser. In *Clinical work with substance-abusing clients*, edited by S. L. A. Straussner. New York: Guilford Press.

Goode, E. 1993. *Drugs in American society*. New York: McGraw Hill.

Greenwood, P. 1992. Substance abuse problems among high-risk youth and potential interventions. *Crime and Delinquency* 38, no. 4:444–58.

Grob, C., and M. D. DeRios. 1992. Adolescent drug use in cross-cultural perspective. *The Journal of Drug Issues* 22, no. 1:121–39.

Hahn, E. J., L. A. Hall, M. K. Rayens, A. V. Burt, D. Corley, and K. L. Sheffel. 2000. Kindergarten children's knowledge and perceptions of alcohol, tobacco, and other drugs. *Journal of School Health* 70:51–55.

Hansen, W. B. 1989. *Prevention program guide: A manual for the uniform evaluation of school-based drug and alcohol prevention programs*. Winston Salem, N.C.: Bowman-Gray School of Medicine.

Harding, C. G., L. A. Safer, J. Kavanagh, R. Bania, L. Carty, L. Lisnov, and K. Wysockey. 1996. Using live theater combined with role-playing and discussion to examine what at-risk adolescents think about substance abuse, its consequences, and prevention. *Adolescence* 31:783–96.

Hawkins, D. J., and R. Catalano. 1992. *Communities that care: Action for drug abuse prevention*. San Francisco, Calif.: Jossey-Bass.

Heineman, A. W. 1993. *Substance abuse and physical disability*. New York: Haworth Press.

Johnson, C. A. 1986. Objectives of community programs to prevent drug abuse. *Journal of School Health* 56:364–68.

Johnson, C. A., et al. 1990. Relative effectiveness of comprehensive community programming for drug abuse prevention with high-risk and low-risk adolescents. *Journal of Consulting and Clinical Psychology* 58, no. 4.

Johnston, L. D., P. M. O'Malley, and J. G. Bachman.1998. *Drug use among American school students, college students, and other young adults: National trends through 1985.* Washington, D.C.: U.S. Government Printing Office.

Kandel, D. B. 1984. Marijuana users in young adulthood. *Archives General Psychiatry* 41:200–209.

Kaplin, S. 1996. Drug prevention with young people: Defining the model and evaluating effects. *Journal of the Institute of Health Education* 34, no. 4.

Kay, J., and J. Cohen. 1998. *The parents' complete guide to young people and drugs.* London: Vermilion.

Kelker, K. A. 1990. School services for drug-addicted children: What parents need to know. *Preventing School Failure* 34, no. 3:22–24.

King, K. A., D. I. Wagner, and B. Hedrick. 2001. Safe and drug-free school coordinators: Perceived needs to improve violence and drug prevention programs. *Journal of School Health* 71:236–41.

Kumpfer, K. L. 1992. Prevention of alcohol and drug abuse: A critical review of risk factors ad prevention strategies. In *Prevention of mental disorders, alcohol and other drug use in children and adolescents,* edited by D. Shafer, I. Philips, and N. Enzer. Washington, D.C.: U.S. Department of Health and Human Services. DHHS Publication no. ADM 92-1646, 00 309–71.

Law Enforcement News. 1996. When it comes to the young, antidrug efforts are going to pot. *Law Enforcement News* 22:441–47.

National Clearinghouse for Alcohol and Drug Information. 1997. Innovative preventive strategies target minority populations. *Prevention Alert* 1, no. 7:1–12.

National Institute on Drug Abuse. 1997. *Drug abuse prevention for at-risk groups.* Washington, D.C.: U.S. Department of Health and Human Services. NIH Publication no. 97-414.

Newcomb, M. 1995. Identifying high-risk youth: Prevalence and patterns of adolescent drug use. In *Adolescent drug abuse: Clinical assessment and therapeutic interventions,* edited by E. Rahdert and D. Czechowicz, 7–38. Washington, D.C.: U.S. Department of Health and Human Services. NIH Publication no. 96-113949.

Nineteenth Annual Report to Congress on the Implementation of Individual with Disabilities Education Act. 1997. Washington, D.C.: U.S. Department of Education.

Oetting, E. R., and F. Beauvais. 1988. *Common elements in youth drug abuse: Peer clusters and other psychosocial factors, in Peele's visions of addiction.* New York: Lexington.

Peele, S. 1996. *Don't panic! A parent's guide to understanding and preventing alcohol and drug abuse.* New York: Lindesmith Center.

Pentz, M. A. 1986. Community organization and school liaisons: How to get programs started. *Journal of School Health* 56:382–88.

Perry, C. L. 1986. Community-wide health promotion and drug abuse prevention. *Journal of School Health* 56:359–63.

Schinke, S. P., G. J. Botvin, and M. A. Orlandi. 1991. *Substance abuse in children and adolescents: Evaluation and intervention.* Newbury Park, Calif.: Sage Publications.

Segal, B., and J. C. Steward. 1996. Substance use and abuse in adolescence: An overview. *Child Psychiatry and Human Development* 26, no. 4:193–210.

St. Pierre, T. L., D. Kaltreider, et al. 1992. Drug prevention in a community setting: A longitudinal study of the relative effectiveness of a three-year primary prevention program in boys and girls clubs across the nation. *American Journal of Community Psychology* 20, no. 6:673–706.

Swan, N. 1995. Targeting prevention messages: Research on drug-use risk and protective factors is fueling the design of ethnically appropriate prevention programs for children. *NIDA Notes* 10, no. 1:1–3.

Taylor, G. R. 1997. *Curriculum strategies: Social skills intervention for young African-American males.* Westport, Conn.: Praeger.

Temple, M., and K. M. Fillmore. 1986. The variability of drinking patterns and problems among young men, age sixteen to thirty-one: A longitudinal study. *International Journal of Addiction* 20: 1595–620.

U.S. Department of Health and Human Services. 1993. *Young teens: Who they are and how to communicate with them about alcohol and other drugs.* Rockville, Md.: U.S. Department of Health and Human Services. Substance Abuse and Mental Health Administration, Center for Substance Abuse.

———. 1998. *Tobacco use among U.S. racial/ethnic minority groups-African American, American Indians, and Alaska Natives, Asian Americans and Pacific Islanders and Hispanics.* A report of the Surgeon General, Centers for Disease Control and Prevention, National Center for Chronic Disease Prevention ad Health Promotion, Office on Smoking and Health. Washington, D.C.: U.S. Department of Health and Human Services.

U.S. General Accounting Office. 1990. *Drug education: School-based programs seen as useful but impact unknown.* Report to the Chairman, Committee on Governmental Affairs, U. S. Senate. Washington, D.C.: U.S. General Accounting Office.

———. 1993. *Drug use among youth: No simple answers to guide prevention.* Washington, D.C.: U.S. General Accounting Office.

Webb, W. 1993. Cognitive behavior therapy with children of alcoholics. *School Counselors* 40:170–77.

White, D., and M. Pitts. 1998. Educating young people about drugs: A systematic review. *Addiction* 93, no. 10:1475–87.

Winters, P. A. 1990. Getting high: Components of successful drug education programs. *Journal of Alcohol and Drug Education* 35, no. 2:20–23.

2

DRUG TREATMENT TECHNIQUES

Research concerning drug treatment techniques is well reported throughout the literature. Some of the treatment modalities are based upon the medical, therapeutic, or psychosocial models. In my view, the medical and psychological treatment methods are beyond the scope of the schools and have been adequately covered elsewhere (Carroll, Nich, Ball, McCance, and Rounsavile 1998; McCance, Elinore, and Kosten 1998; O'Farrell and Feehan 1999; Miller 1995; Wolfe and Meyers 1999). Treatment modalities within the psychosocial areas appear to be within the purview of the schools and are addressed in this chapter.

PSYCHOSOCIAL TREATMENT TECHNIQUES

The twelve-step abstinence treatment is based upon the principles advocated by Alcoholic Anonymous (AA). This program is based on the concept that alcoholism is an addiction to alcohol and is considered an independent disease or disorder (Laundergan 1982; O'Farrell and Feehan 1999; Finney, Moos, and Humphreys 1999). Research findings reported by these authors, however, tend to argue that the twelve-step model has not been effective in reducing substance abuse, other than alcohol abuse.

This chapter proposes to examine the research related to psychosocial interventions to reduce substance abuse. The proposed model is based upon behavioral techniques and principles derived from learning theory, specifically from Bandura's Social Learning Theory, and includes social learning, motivation, imitation, modeling, and coping behaviors (Bandura and Walters 1963; Bandura 1977). Research findings concerning the effectiveness of this approach in reducing substance abuse have generally been positive among youths.

This chapter outlines specific strategies that have proven successful in combating the drug problems of youths. Some of these methods include motivational interviewing, social skills training, behavior contracting, peer mediation, cognitive behavior intervention, self-control training, and group counseling.

MOTIVATIONAL INTERVIEWING

According to Bien, Miller, and Boroughs (1993); Brown and Miller (1990); Miller (1983); Rollnick, Heather, and Bell (1992), and Clayton, Cattarello, and Johnstone (1996), motivational interviewing is designed to assist individuals in making behavior changes between indulgence and restraint. It may be defined, for educational purposes, as a directive student-centered counseling style for assisting students in exploring alternatives to taking drugs. The technique involves administrators and educators using nondirective and self-directed counseling skills, eliciting self-motivating remarks, listening carefully to students, evaluating their desire to change and, at an opportune time, choosing the appropriate moment to explore motivation. Questions concerning drug usage or the likes and dislike of drug usage may be posed to the students (Miller and Rollnick 1991).

SOCIAL SKILLS TRAINING

Social skills training has been used successfully in several disciplines to change or modify behavior. Its major thrust involves instructing individuals to form and maintain interpersonal relationships (Taylor 1997;

Hedley, Houtz, and Baratta 1990; Channey 1989). Most children can learn from receiving rewards and punishments and then proceed to make a judgment in new social situations. Components of the strategy frequently include the following skills: (1) communication, (2) listening, (3) problem solving, (4) and assertiveness. Social skills training should not be considered as a singular treatment for maladaptive behavior, but rather as an adjunct to treatment. Principles of social skills training have been applied to treat many types of drug addictions.

Lack of social skills may interfere with successful treatment of addicts by impeding interpersonal relationships in peer groups. Students must be taught how to exhibit behaviors that will demonstrate how to successfully cope with peer pressure concerning the use of drugs. Through the use of social referencing (involving using information from other individuals to guide behavior), positive peer relations can be a powerful ally in combating drug usage among students. Through social skills training and employing peer interactions, the harmful affects of drugs may be demonstrated by permitting students to verbalize their feelings, develop appropriate problem-solving techniques, and become cognizant of how to say no to drugs (Oldenberg 1998; Heilig and Rosenbaum 1999).

BEHAVIOR CONTRACTING

With behavior contracting, the educator/administrator, student, and parent discuss and develop standards or clear contingencies for changing behaviors related to using drugs. The final product is usually a written contract specifying the types and kinds of reinforcers that will be given to the student if he or she refrains from engaging in drugs. This strategy is also referred to as contingency management and has been successfully used in the treatment of drug abuse.

Additionally, it may be employed to provide educators with strategies for assisting students in viewing drugs as inappropriate. There are several ways in which drug behaviors can be modified. Contingency contracting, a task-centered approach, and peer mediation are three of the most promising techniques used to reduce drug abuse (Horn, Rude, and Keillor 1999; Higgins and Silverman 1999).

Contingency Contracting

This technique involves pupils in planning and executing drug contracts. Gradually, students take over keeping their own records concerning drug usage. Teachers and parents carefully monitor the process. The student agrees to limit his or her intake for specific time periods until the habit is eradicated. If the agreed contract is followed, the student receives a tangible reward that is designed to impede drug usage (Higgins and Silverman 1999).

Task-Centered Approach

The task-centered approach is another way to reduce drug usage among students. Students may be experiencing difficulty with drugs because they fail to grasp the long-term, harmful effects of using them. Activities should be structured for students to work independently or in groups in a well-controlled learning environment addressing how drug usage may be controlled.

Peer Mediation Strategies

Peer mediation strategies have been successfully employed to manage drug behavior. The model is student driven and enables students to make decisions about issues involving using drugs. The model requires that the students exercise self-regulation strategies that will assist them in internalizing the harmful effects of using drugs. Once brought to the conscious level, students may be able to control their drug habits. The use of models, coaching, role-playing, cueing, films, filmstrips, and videotapes will facilitate the process.

Cognitive-Behavior Intervention

These techniques focus on having individuals think about and internalize their feelings and behaviors before reacting. The process involves learning responses from the environment by listening, observing, and imitating others. Cognitive behavior interventions are designed to increase self-control of behavior through self-monitoring, self-evaluation, and self-reinforcement, and assist students in comparing their drug behaviors against predetermined standards imposed by peers relevant to substance abuse. Recent research findings imply that incorporation of a cognitive-behavioral intervention within the school curriculum may have some impact on preventing adolescents from using drugs (Botvin, Baker, et al. 1990; Brayer 1970, 53; Rosen 1975; Finney, Moos, and Humphreys 1999).

SELF-CONTROL TRAINING

Harris and Miller (1990), Hester and Miller (1989), and Taylor (1997) all agreed that self-control training can be effectively conducted by nontherapeutic personnel, such as teachers and educators. Accordingly, the training involves teaching students self-management skills designed to reduce drug intake. Common elements of the strategy include goal setting, self-monitoring, rage control and reduction, self-reinforcement of progress, assessing goal achievement, functional analysis, and learning coping skills.

Collectively, the authors articulated that self-control training appears to be effective only for those individuals with less severe alcohol and drug problems. This description fits many students in our public schools. If recognized early enough, and with the help of competent personnel and support, many students can be saved from a life of drug abuse.

Some recommended strategies to employ in teaching students to control their actions toward drugs are:

1. Educators should seek to develop forms of self-control among students who encourage nonjudgmental behaviors that glamorize drugs.
2. Instruction in drug education should focus more on metacognitive activities, where students are taught to internally analyze their behaviors before they act.
3. Activities should be designed that teach children to be responsible for their own behavior relevant to drug abuse by using self-regulation strategies.

GROUP COUNSELING

For the purpose of this chapter, group counseling is defined as a collection of individuals who come together to identify, assess, discuss, or evaluate common problems or tasks facing the group. The major task is to work on each member's specific drug problem. In a broad sense, groups should always be therapeutic (Vannicelli 1982; Khantzian, Halliday, and McAuliffe 1990; Denning 1998). Group counseling tends to be therapeutic because:

1. It gives the feeling that individuals are not alone and instills hope that their conditions will improve.
2. Group members offer support and ideas.
3. Students learn from their interactions and relationships in the group by watching others who are experiencing similar problems.
4. It promotes and encourages self-efficacy.
5. It maintains confidentiality.
6. All issues are discussed seriously.
7. Members can assess the evidence of drug use and recovery.
8. It can introduce individuals to various types of intervention techniques.
9. It can provide strategies for individuals to set realistic goals.
10. It can assist individuals in assessing their strengths and weaknesses toward substance abuse.
11. It can reduce levels of self-pity and defensiveness (Flores 1988).

Group counselors should be empathic and skilled in counseling techniques when conducting counseling sessions (Lowinson, Ruiz, Millman, and Langrod 1997). They should be appraised of drug problems in the group. Motivational interviewing may be used to assess drug problems, as indicated earlier in the chapter. They should arrive early and have the room ready. When conducting counseling sessions, the following are recommended:

1. Be on time and well prepared.
2. Express curiosity about every aspect of the students' drug experiences.

3. Do not force students to talk about substance use; try to encourage the students to believe in and trust the group.
4. Maintain neutrality regarding students' drug use and goals.
5. Educate when needed.
6. Understand and roll with resistance within the group.
7. Manage counter transference within the group.
8. Permit students to teach and instruct.
9. Share responsibilities among the group (Flores 1988).

INTERDISCIPLINARY APPROACH

Intervention strategies related to drug abuse in the schools are frequently used to eliminate or reduce the use of drugs by employing various kinds of behavioral interventions (White and Pitts 1994); Taylor 1972; Thomas 1969; Thomas and Bowen 1969). Educators must use adequate preparation and sensitivity when employing psychological and behavioral interventions. It is recommended that an initial interview be arranged with the student to secure a history of the problem and to determine a rigid schedule for the intervention. In some cases, problems may be too involved for educators to deal with successfully. In cases of this magnitude, an interdisciplinary approach may be needed. The student may be referred to resources outside of the school. See chapters 5 and 7 for specific details on employing an interdisciplinary approach.

Direct intervention by the schools is considered to be of prime interest, because national statistics indicate that addiction to hard drugs is on the increase among youths (Cohen 1995; Goode 1993; Johnston, O'Malley, and Bachman 1998; Samhs 1989; U.S. Department of Health and Human Services 1993). The exact number of students using drugs is not known because many of them are not apprehended or convicted. The increase in drug abuse may be attributed to many factors; many are deep rooted in the cultures and various types of personality conflicts that youth experience in our society. Chapter 5 explores this issue in greater detail.

Regardless of the factors that contribute to an increase in drug usage, one key to breaking the vicious drug cycle is the education of students. Such education should be directed toward prevention of drug use and

rehabilitation of drug users, with an emphasis on the causes and consequences of drug misuse and abuse.

Miller's (1983) research revealed that counselors who employed directive versus nondirective treatment found no difference in drug intake. However, there were differences when individuals used high levels of empathy; outcomes were significantly better. Note that being
empathetic does not imply that the counselor is nondirective or non-
confrontational. An effective interventionist can be both and confrontational and at the same time be empathetic. When all of these components are evident, the interventionist is reflecting motivational
interviewing in its best form. Miller and Rollnick wrote that research
findings on this style of intervention imply that it is a promising alternative to a hostile, aggressive style of confrontation as a way to motivate individuals to change (1991, 40). Before any change can be promoted,
counselors or educators and students develop a mutually agreed-upon
goal. A first step in the process is for the interventionist or educator to
conduct an objective assessment of the student's alcohol/drug habits.
Motivational strategies are then planned to reduce the drug habit. Reduction of a drug habit can only occur when the student is permitted to
select a goal in concert with his or her own values (Brown 1995, 1997;
Ching 1981; Peele 1986; White and Pitts 1994).

There are mixed reactions toward using ex-addicts in drug education
programs. Some educators feel that ex-addicts will turn students to the
use of drugs by glamorizing the effects; others believe that ex-addicts
who have gone through the system are better equipped to give students
firsthand information that will deglamorize drug usage, appealing to the
student's own value system and his or her assessment of what physical,
social, and psychological damages might result from using drugs. The
technique of employing ex-addicts as discussion leaders with high school
students is viable. They can create an atmosphere conducive to raising
questions that might not have been asked in a structured classroom setting.

Although it is felt that ex-addicts can contribute significantly to a drug
education program, it is highly recommended that they receive intensive in-service training under the supervision of qualified personnel; be
carefully chosen; and be given complete medical, physical, and psychological examinations before working with youths (California State De-

partment of Education 1968, 16–27). The notion of ex-addicts working under the direct supervision of the teacher in planning and instructing youths about drugs is highly endorsed.

Educators should be aware that alcohol is a major "gateway" leading to drug usage and that much drug usage is attributed to peer pressure, cultural factors, poor parental role models who use illegal drugs, severe impulsivity, and rebellious behavior. The effect of peer pressure appears to be paramount on students and frequently more powerful than parental or community factors (Grob and DeRios 1992; Duncan 1991; Ponton 1997). Recent research findings have clearly shown a significant relationship between antisocial behavior and substance abuse. The research did not indicate whether the association between antisocial behavior and drug usage is causal, or that one disorder leads to the other. In essence, does antisocial behavior promote substance abuse or does substance abuse promote antisocial behavior (Robin 1998; Vanden Bree, Svikis, and Pickens 1998)?

Appropriate models must be used to demonstrate to students how to say no. Other strategies should be designed to address the other factors articulated above (Botvin, Baker, Filazzola, et al. 1990; Hanson 1996; Heilig and Rosebaum 1999; Oldenberg 1998).

SUMMARY

It is incumbent upon educators using psychosocial intervention strategies to first assess what types of treatment work best for the students. If treatment modalities are not matched with assessed needs of students, the effectiveness of the treatment may be in doubt.

Research reported in this chapter tends to support the following premises:

1. There is no one best psychosocial intervention treatment; the selected psychosocial intervention treatment works best when matched with assessed needs.
2. Drug programs should offer a variety of treatments.
3. Educators or interventionists should be trained and competent in the intervention used.

4. The characteristics of interventionists, particularly empathy, should be considered when selecting them for training.
5. Different techniques should be evident for encouraging children from different cultural backgrounds to abstain from using drugs.
6. The role of ex-addicts in drug education, although encouraged, should be carefully assessed.
7. Modeling and peer relationships are powerful allies in promoting or decreasing drug usage.
8. Successful drug treatment programs involve the total school, parents, and the community.

REFERENCES

Bandura, A. 1977. *Social learning theory*. Englewood Cliffs, N.J.: Prentice-Hall.

Bandura, A., and R. Walters. 1963. *Social learning and personality development*. New York: Rinehart and Winston.

Bien, T., W. Miller, and J. Boroughs. 1993. Motivational interviewing with alcohol outpatients. *Behavioral Psychotherapy* 21:347–56.

Botvin, G. J., E. Baker, A. D. Filazzola, et al. 1990. A cognitive behavioral approach to substance abuse prevention: One-year follow-up. *Addict Behavior* 15:47–63.

Brayer, H. O. 1968. *A comparative analysis of drug use and its relationship to certain attitudes, values and cognitive knowledge on drugs between eighth and eleventh grade students in the Coronado Unified School Districts*. Coronado, Calif.: Unified School District.

Brown, J., and W. R. Miller. 1993. Impact of motivational interviewing on participation and outcome in residential alcoholism treatment. *Psychology of Addictive Behaviors* 7:21–218.

Brown, J. H. 1995. *Tuning out and turning on: Student response to contemporary drug education*. New York: Lindesmith Center. Audiotape of seminar presentation

———. 1997. Listen to the kids. *American School Board Journal* 184:38–47.

Carroll, K. M., C. Nich, S. A. Ball, E. McCance, and B. J. Rounsavile. 1998. *Addiction* 93, no. 5:713–27.

Channey, E. F. 1989. Social skills training. In *Handbook of Alcoholism Treatment*, edited by R. K. Haster and W. R. Miller. New York: Pergamon Press.

Ching, C. L. 1981. The goal of abstinence: Implications for drug education. *Journal of Drug Education* 11, no. 1:13–18.

Clayton, R. R., A. M. Cattarello, and B. M. Johnstone. 1996. The effectiveness of drug abuse resistance education (Project D.A.R.E.): Five-year follow-up results. *Preventive Medicine* 25:307–18.

Cohen, J. 1995. *Drugs*. London: Evans.

Denning, P. 1998. Therapeutic interventions for individuals with substance use, HIV, and personality disorders: Harm reduction as a unifying approach. In *Psychotherapy in Practice*. Vol. 4, 37–52. New York: Wiley.

Duncan, D. F. 1991. Problems associated with three commonly used drugs: A survey of rural secondary school student. *Psychology of Addictive Behavior* 5 no. 2:93–96.

Finney, J. W., R. H. Moose, and K. Humphreys. 1999a. A comparative evaluation of substance abuse treat: Eleven linking potential outcomes of twelve-step and cognitive-behavioral treatment to substance use outcomes. *Clinical and Experimental Research* 23, no. 3:537–44.

———. 1999b. Alcoholism. *Clinical and Experimental Research* 23, no. 3:532–44.

Flores, P. 1988. Characteristics of the leader. In *Group psychotherapy with addicted population*. New York: Haworth Press.

Goode, E. 1993. *Drugs in American society*. New York: McGraw-Hill.

Grob, C., and M. D. DeRios. 1992. Adolescent drug use in cross-cultural perspective. *The Journal of Drug Issues* 22, no. 1:121–39.

Hanson, D. L. 1996. *Alcohol education: What we must do*. Westport, Conn.: Praeger Publishers.

Harris, K. B., and W. R. Miller. 1990. Behavioral self-control training for problem Drinkers: Components of efficacy. *Psychology of Addictive Behavior* 4:82–90.

Hedley, C., J. Houtz, and A. Baratta. 1990. *Cognition, curriculum, and literacy*. Norwood, N.J.: Ablex Publishing.

Heilig, S., and M. Rosenbaum. 1999. *Teens and drugs: Time to just say no*. San Francisco, Calif.: San Francisco Medicine.

Hester, R. K., and W. R. Miller. 1989. Self-control training. In *Handbook of Alcoholism Treatment Approaches: Effective Alternatives*. Elmford, N.Y.: Pergamon Press.

Higgins, S. T., and K. Silverman. 1999. Motivating behavior change among illicit drug abusers. *Research on Contingency Management Interventions*. Washington, D.C.: American Psychological Association.

Horn, J. J., S. S. Rude, and R. M. Keillor. 1999. Substance use disorders. In *Handbook of prescriptive treatments for children and adolescents*. 2nd ed., edited by R. T. Ammerman, M. Hersen, et al., 229–43. Boston, Mass.: Allyn and Bacon.

Johnston, L. D., P. M. O'Malley, and J. G. Bachman. 1998. *National survey results on drug use from Monitoring the Future study.* Rockville, Md.: Human Services.

Khantzian, E., K. S. Halliday, and W. E. McAuliffe. 1990. *Addiction and the vulnerable self: Modified dynamic group therapy for substance abusers.* New York: Guilford Press.

Laundergan, J. C. 1982. *Easy does it. Alcoholism treatment outcomes: Hazelden and the Minnesota Model.* Center City, Minn.: Hazelden Foundation.

Lowinson, J. H., P. Ruiz, R. B. Millman, and J. G. Langrod, eds. 1997. *Substance abuse: A comprehensive textbook.* Baltimore, Md.: Williams and Wilkie.

McCance, K., F. Elinore, and T. R. Kosten. 1998. *New treatments for chemical additions.* Washington, D.C.: American Psychiatric Press.

Miller, N. S. 1995. *History and review of contemporary addiction treatment.* New York: Haworth Press.

Miller, W. R. 1983. Motivational interviewing with problem drinkers. *Behavioral Psychotherapy* 11:147–72.

———. 1994. Motivational interviewing: III. On the ethics of motivational intervention. *Behavioral and Cognitive Psychotherapy* 22:111–23.

Miller, W. R., and S. C. Rollnick. 1991. *Motivational interviewing: Preparing people to change addictive behavior.* New York: Guilford Press.

O'Farrell, T. J., and M. Feehan. 1999. Alcoholism treatment and the family: Do family and individual treatments for alcoholic adults have preventive effects on children? *Journal of Studies on Alcohol* 13:125–29.

Oldenberg, D. 1998. Kids and alcohol: A controversial alternative to just say no. *Washington Post,* 10 March.

Peele, S. 1986. The "cure" for adolescent drug abuse: Worse than the problem? *Journal of Counseling and Development* 65:23–24.

Ponton, L. 1997. *The romance of risk: Why teenagers do the things they do?* New York: Basic Books.

Robin, L. N. 1998. The intimate connection between antisocial personality and substance abuse. *Social Psychiatry and Psychiatric Epidemiology* 33, no. 8:393–99.

Rollnick, S., N. Heather, and A. Bell. 1992. Negotiating behavior change in medical settings: The development of brief motivational interviewing. *Journal of Mental Health* 1:25–37.

Rosen, M. J. 1970. *An evaluative study comparing the cognitive and attitudinal effects of two versions of an educational program about mind-affecting drugs.* San Francisco, Calif.: Evaluation and Research Associates.

Samhs, A. 1989. *Office of Applied Studies, National Household Survey on Drug Abuse: Main findings*. Washington, D.C.: National Clearinghouse for Alcohol and Drug Information.

Taylor, G. R. 1972. Toward a model K–12 program in drug education. *Thrust for Educational Leadership* 1, no. 4:28–32.

———. 1997. *Curriculum strategies: Social skills intervention for young African American males*. Westport, Conn.: Praeger Press.

Thomas, U. 1969. *Drugs and the educational process*. Washington, D.C.: American Foundation of Psychiatry.

Thomas, U., and H. Bowen. 1969. *Drug abuse and the schools*. Washington, D.C.: American Foundation of Psychiatry.

Vanden Bree, M. B. N., D. S. Svikis, and R. W. Pickens. 1998. Genetic influences in antisocial personality and drug use disorders. *Drug and Alcohol Dependency* 49, no. 3:177–87.

Vannicelli, M. 1982. Group psychotherapy with alcoholics: Special techniques. *Journal Studies on Alcoholism* 42:17–37.

White, D., and M. Pitts. 1994. Educating young people about drugs: A systematic review. *Addiction* 93, no. 10:1475–87.

Wolfe, B. L., and R. J. Meyers. 1999. Cost-effective alcohol treatment: The community reinforcement approach. *Cognitive and Behavioral Practice* 6, no. 2:105–9.

3

COLLABORATIVE PLANNING
IN DRUG EDUCATION

Collaboration between school, parents, and community is necessary to plan a comprehensive drug curriculum. Community, student, and parental input ensures, to a larger extent, the success of the program. Collaborative efforts may be improved through formulating teams to set realistic goals, identify physical and human resources, assess the needs of the community, and develop a realistic and functional curriculum. You must build in an effective evaluation design that measures more than drug knowledge, while at the same time changing attitudes and behaviors of drug usage (Fox, Forbing, and Anderson 1988).

Parental and community support are necessary for successful drug curricula. A first step may be to develop school–community teams. These stakeholders may be teachers, parents, students, local community agencies, and businesses, as well as local, state, and federal agencies involved in drug prevention. A second step would be for the team to develop realistic objectives that will have an impact on drug use. A third step should involve a needs assessment in order to identify problems, the characteristics of the community, and human and physical resources (Fox, Forbing, and Anderson 1988). Questionnaires, surveys, and interviews may be used to gather information. Information of this nature is essential in developing an effective drug education program. A fourth step will be for the team to use the assessment data to develop an age-appropriate curriculum that identifies symptoms of drug use, factors associated with dependency, activities and strategies to reduce drug usage, social and cultural factors associated with drugs, and legal and medical aspects of drugs (Goode 1991; Milgram 1987; National School Safety Center 1988; U.S. Department of Education 1990a). Finally, a fifth step for the team will be a need to develop an evaluation designed to measure the effectiveness of the curriculum. (Refer to chapter 9 for a detailed evaluation design.)

The schools cannot by themselves be expected to rehabilitate youth and their neighborhood environments. Sociologists and others who have worked in the drug-abuse prevention field have pointed out that drug education is not a problem for the schools alone. It is a community problem and requires total community effort for its solution. The schools cannot assume the roles of parents, clergymen, enforcement officers, physicians, or psychiatrists—but they can exercise leadership in facing a problem that the total community, working together, can try to remedy. This is education in its broadest and most important sense. It is making schools relevant to their communities. Schools should recognize the many positive contributions that parents and the community can contribute to drug education (Orlandi 1986).

An initial effort must be made to formulate school policies that are sensitive to the needs of all elements of the school community. There is no point, for example, in expecting uninhibited class discussions or adult cooperation when student informers are widely used throughout the school and teachers are required to report all suspected users to the police. If the school intends to act as an extension of civil authority, to investigate and turn users over to the police, it must come to terms with the fact that its effectiveness as an educational force will be substantially reduced. On the other hand, no school administrator can be expected to sit idly by while drug traffic flourishes within the school. Therefore, a major responsibility of school authorities is to give careful consideration to alternative choices in defining the school's action policy toward drug use. Once established, the policy should be clearly explained to students and their parents, as well as to the school staff. The failure of school administrators to communicate with students about policies that they will be expected to obey inevitably creates mistrust of all official advice and information. By seeking and accepting input from young people and their parents in the formulation of school policies, school officials not only open up valuable channels of communication but make it possible to develop policies that are relevant to the needs, interests, and aspirations of each member of the school community (Campo and Rohner 1992; Komro, Perry, Veblen-Mortenson, and Williams 1994).

Dissatisfied with past results, many school systems are trying a variety of new preventive-educational methods to discourage drug abuse, involving more direction by the students themselves (McGovern and Dupont 1991; Palmer and Ringwalt 1988). The New York City Board of Education announced a trial program in sixteen high schools in which pupils will design and run their own antidrug programs. In Philadelphia, selected students from seven high schools (accompanied by a teacher) learned basic drug facts from doctors, treatment experts, and law-enforcement officials and went on field trips. They then went back to their own schools to initiate and run programs of their own choice. Most of them opened counseling services. With regard to peer involvement, there are indications that students should be given a voice in basic approach, curriculum content, and choice of teachers, but should not be saddled with administrative chores, which they abhor and often perform poorly. Nevertheless, tapping the enthusiasm of well-selected students can be beneficial in motivating the student body to seek creative antidrug activities (Moore 1993; Nelson-Simley and Erickson 1995). Students, parents, and community needs must be considered in planning a drug curriculum. Instruments should be designed to elicit stakeholders' attitudes toward the use of drugs and the danger of drugs. Results should be used to help construct a drug program based upon these needs.

Peer group membership has a significant impact on youths taking drugs (Klepp, Halper, and Perry 1986). Youths may not accept drugs initially but rather share a cluster of values and beliefs that make substance abuse attractive. These values and beliefs may eventually lead the youths to taking drugs (Mounts and Steinberg 1995). Stimmel's (1993) findings support the above premise. He contended that drug-related behavior is strongly associated with drug experimentation among friends. Peer influence reaches its peak during early adolescence and manifests itself significantly with the use of marijuana and cigarette smoking.

The notion that young people relate to their peers better than to adults has validity but also limits. They relate only to some of their peers. Rigid social groups exist in many schools, and students chosen by teachers and school officials may not be the ones to lead the group that the antidrug program hopes most to reach. Whenever possible, some student participation in planning and operating programs should come from the group the program is trying to reach, whether nonusers, experimenters, or borderline cases. The student council in an Oregon high school sought the cooperation of ex-users and faculty in creating a youthful "Mod Squad." Teams of experienced students provided successful peer counseling, assistance in crisis situations, and referrals to local treatment facilities, and otherwise contributed positively to the school's educational programming (Dielman, Kloska, Leech, Schulenberg, and Shope 1992; Dobkin, Tremblay, Masse, and Vitaro 1995). In developing goals, Goal 6 of the National Goals 1990 should be consulted.

Goal 6 of the National Goals 1990 focused on "Safe, Disciplined, and Drug-Free Schools." (Refer to appendix B for specific details.) This goal stated that by the year 2000, every school in America would be free of drugs and violence and would offer a disciplined environment conducive to learning (National Commission on Drug Free Schools 1990). Many attempts have been made to achieve this goal. Several school districts have experimented with comprehensive drug prevention programs. In some instances, programs have been infused with health and physical education programs; in other instances, separate drug prevention programs have been developed (Fox, Forbing, and Anderson 1988; Goodstadt 1986; Tricker and Davis 1988; U.S. Department of Education 1990b; Dade County Public Schools 1989; Austin Independent School District 1989).

Collective data from these studies have clearly shown in 2002 that Goal 6 has not been achieved. In a recent survey, 19 percent of high school seniors indicated that they had smoked cigarettes, and 9 percent had drunk alcohol by sixth grade; half of eighth graders had smoked cigarettes, and 77 percent reported having used alcohol and slightly over half of twelfth graders reported at least one experience with illicit drugs. One result of this experience is that it may lead to youths being infected with HIV. As a result, drug education should be infused and integrated into other content areas (National Commission on Drug Free Schools 1990).

In order to move forward in achieving the goals articulated in 1990, school systems and districts must have well-developed plans consisting of:

1. assessing and identifying prevention strategies based upon the uniqueness of the community;
2. providing in-service training for all stakeholders;
3. incorporating parents and the community in developing, implementing, coordinating, adopting, and modifying the program as evaluative results indicate;
4. identifying funding sources.

Refer to sources cited earlier in the chapter and to chapter 5; use the goals and objectives of the program to determine whether they have been achieved. Revise program as data indicate. Achieving goals and developing programs can be expensive; educators will have to plan for financial assistance.

FINANCING DRUG EDUCATION

Safe and Drug-Free Schools and Communities Act

The federal government spends $2 billion annually for research and program support, with nearly $4 billion in total annual spending nationwide on drug education research and program support.

The latest pressure on school-based drug education programs comes from federal legislation. Congress enacted the Drug-Free Schools and Communities Act in 1987 (and many subsequent amendments) to strengthen our nation's drug education and prevention programs. Effective July 1, 1988, local school districts were to be expected, for the first time, to provide evidence of program effectiveness in order to receive federal Title IV funds.

The 1994 Safe and Drug-Free Schools and Communities Act (SDFSCA) delineated opportunities for alternative approaches in favor of these educational programs. The defects in D.A.R.E. were not revealed in its annual evaluation. The act failed to live up to its mandate, "that by year 2000, all schools in America will be free of drugs and violence." Research findings demonstrate that the recommendations have not been found to be effective (Silvia and Thorne 1997).

Effective July 1, 2002, the SDFSCA State Grants (subpart 1) program authorizes a variety of activities designed to prevent school violence and youth drug use, and to help schools and communities create

safe, disciplined, and drug-free environments that support student academic achievement. One of the significant changes in the SDFSCA is
a requirement that state and local prevention programs and activities
meet the "Principles of Effectiveness." Under the reauthorized SDF-
SCA, the principles of effectiveness include a requirement that funds
be used to support only programs grounded in scientifically based research (www.ed.gov/offices/OSDFS/sdfscaguidance_12_02.doc).

On January 2, 2003, the Education Department issued nonregulatory
draft guidance for state and local implementation of programs under Title IV, Part A, Subpart 1 of the SDFSCA. The SDFSCA is a crucial part
of President Bush's national effort to ensure academic success for all
students.

Funding is widely available for research-based strategies that are
consistent with the new principles of effectiveness. One of the core
principles is that a program must be effective in preventing or reducing drug use, violence, or disruptive behavior (Silvia and Thorne 1997).
The new SDFSCA language will force many states, school districts, and
schools to give more attention to drug education goals, processes, and
evaluation results. If proposed school-based programs are taken at face
value, their main goal is clear—to prevent drug use among the target
population. Whether programs can achieve this goal is an empirical
question that should be answered, in part, through rigorous evaluation
research.

Other federal funding sources include competitive grants, under
ESEA Title IV part A, Subpart 2, Sections 415 and 412 National Coor-
dinator Program, designed for local education agencies to apply for
funds to combat substance abuse. The federal government provides
many funding resources for local and state education agencies. (For a
complete listing of the sources, see the U.S. Department of Education
at www.ed.gov/offices/OSDFS/sdfs. For private funding sources, local
and state educational agencies might consult Business Wire at
www.aegis.com/news/bw/1997/bw970510.html.)

The No Child Left Behind Act

A more recent legislation, the No Child Left Behind Act of 2001
(NCLB) PL-107-110, signed into law by President Bush on January 8,

2002, authorized $650 million in FY2002. Such sums may also be necessary in the succeeding five years for the safe schools state grant programs, which provides grants to school districts to ensure that schools are free of drugs and that schools are safe for all children (www.nochildleftbehind.gov). In adding clarity to PL-107-110, the U.S. Department of Education issued nonregulatory draft guidelines for state and local school districts to follow.

SCHOOL-BASED DRUG PROGRAMS

Drug Abuse Resistance Education (D.A.R.E.) is a series of school-based drug and violence prevention programs for children in kindergarten through twelfth grade. It is a cooperative venture between law enforcement agencies, schools, and the local community, and it involves the use of trained, uniformed police officers in the classroom to teach a carefully planned drug prevention curriculum. Created in 1983 as a collaborative venture between the Los Angeles Police Department and the Los Angeles United School District, D.A.R.E. has expanded to become the largest drug education initiative in the world. The core D.A.R.E. curriculum, which is the subject of this research, focuses on children in their last year of elementary school (fifth or sixth grade). It is based on the assumption that students at this age are the most receptive to antidrug messages as they approach the age of drug experimentation. It is the nation's most popular school-based drug education program, is administered in approximately 70 percent of the nation's school districts, reaching 25 million students in 1996, and has been adopted in forty-four foreign countries (*Law Enforcement News* 1996). Its effectiveness in combating drug usage, however, has been a matter of bitter controversy, and this debate is taking place in the context of rising drug use among our nation's youth. After experiencing large declines in drug use in the 1980s, the national trend began to reverse in the early 1990s: The percentage of high school seniors who reported using illegal drugs "during the past year" increased from 22 percent in 1992 to 35 percent in 1995—a 59 percent increase (Johnston et al. 1996). Marijuana experienced dramatic increases. The number of eighth graders who reported using marijuana during their lifetime jumped from 10.2 percent in 1991 to 19.9 percent in 1995—a 92 percent increase. Reports from the Office of National Drug Control Policy (1997) reflect a growing concern about recent trends in drug use attitudes and behaviors among America's youth, and call upon the nation to act swiftly to prevent a future drug epidemic.

This growing drug problem has caused a flurry of media coverage and political finger pointing, all leading to closer scrutiny of our nation's efforts to control and prevent drug abuse. The spotlight has been especially strong on America's most popular and visible program—D.A.R.E. Whether or not D.A.R.E. has been an effective prevention program has been the subject of considerable debate and research. The publication of a national study that questioned the effectiveness of D.A.R.E. in preventing drug use (Ringwalt et al. 1994; Research Triangle Institute 1994; Aniskiewicz and Wysong 1987; Glass 1988; Rosenbaum, Flewelling, Bailey, Ringwalt and Wilkinson 1994) opened the door to an avalanche of criticism in the popular press. Of course, the problem of demonstrating effectiveness in drug prevention is not unique to D.A.R.E. Several literature reviews and meta-analyses of school-based drug prevention programs have concluded that most are ineffective in preventing drug use (see Battjes 1985; Botvin 1990; Ennett et al. 1994; Hansen and Mc-Neal 1997; Ringwalt et al. 1994; Tobler 1986).

Within the middle school, several programs are available. Students have been trained and are actively involved in conflict resolution and peer mediation programs. These school programs have resulted in the formulation of special groups of students who are active in assisting fellow students when needed (Palmer and Paisley 1991). Many middle schools also conduct an "Awareness Day." This special event utilizes the resources of area health agencies, drug education agencies, and private enterprises. Speakers address students in assemblies and in classroom situations during the day-long process. Students determine speaker topics and each student chooses the classes he or she wishes to attend. Topics may include AIDS; teen suicide; stress; family relationships; communication; alcoholism; drug dependency; steroids and athletics; physical, emotional or social abuse; teen pregnancy; and more. The D.A.R.E. program is presented to all the fifth- and sixth-grade students every other year.

The Life Skills Training (LST) program has reduced cigarette smoking among youths by 40 percent. This percentage was maintained for two years. The program has also been known to reduce the consumption of alcohol and other substance abuse drugs. The program has been revised to be used in community programs, and is claimed by Dusenbury, Botvin, and James (1989) to promote the development of skills in the individual and work to create meaningful roles for adolescents in the environment.

The Community Reinforcement Approach (CRA) is based upon social learning intervention strategies (chapter 5). It integrates several cost-effective treatments for clinicians to use to combat drug usage. Clearly stated objectives guide the extent of the treatment provided (Wolfe and Meyers 1999). Competent staff are needed to conduct treatment modalities.

IN-SERVICE TEACHER EDUCATION

Research conducted by Tricker and Davis (1988) revealed that in-service education is essential for an effective curriculum for both teachers and support staff. A functional and realistic program for teachers should be developed. Workshops designed for one or two days cannot adequately cover the wide gamut of drug problems and will leave little room for innovation. What is needed is an intensive program that extends a week or longer, as well as college-based instruction given for credits. An interdisciplinary approach should be evident for in-service workshops and college-based instruction courses, with many specialists included to cover the wide spectrum of illegal, legal, moral, social, educational, physical, medical, and psychological factors inherent in the problem. An ideal team might consist of the following individuals: a doctor, lawyer, school nurse, teacher, physical education instructor, clergyman, psychologist, and social worker. Research has also shown that in-service training needs differ when presented to experienced and inexperienced teachers. The inexperienced teachers need significantly more information on drugs than their peers. Experienced teachers can profit from working with curriculum materials.

INSTRUCTION IN DRUG EDUCATION

Teaching about drugs is generally best provided as part of an integrated program spanning all four key stages. Many of the attitudes and behaviors are common to other aspects of health education. To single out drug education for separate treatment may risk glamorizing the subject or losing opportunities to reinforce wider messages about healthy lifestyles. However a program of drug education is organized, the essential aim should be to give pupils the facts, emphasize the benefits of a lifestyle, and give young people the knowledge and skills to make informed and responsible choices now and later in life.

Drug education requires sensitive teaching matched to the particular needs and concerns of pupils in the class (Kantor and Caudill 1992). Teachers need to use their professional judgment where the class includes pupils from ethnic minority or religious communities with particular sensitivities. In addition, careful consideration needs to be given to the possibility that pupils' parents or siblings may have experienced drug abuse. This is deemed important if teachers are to respond appropriately to students' impromptu questions concerning drugs.

Teachers should be responsive to changing trends in drug abuse and must offer a credible and consistent message. Teaching about illegal drugs is unlikely to have a lasting effect if a lesson is given in isolation or as a one-off response to a drug-related incident in the school. Teaching approaches that set out to shock or to frighten may actually increase interest and encourage experimentation. However, with the young child aged three to nine, a clear warning about the dangerous effects of drugs can be particularly powerful (Mothers against Misuse and Abuse 1998, 1999; Moore and Saunders 1991).

The teacher is the key person in any instructional program. He or she is more than a vehicle of knowledge. He or she must be equipped to mold students' attitudes and beliefs and create a type of rapport that will elicit students' respect and support. Teachers need a comprehensive knowledge base in drug education; therefore, it is essential that a specialist be available to present information.

Reaction to the presence of a teacher in the room where a drug education program is conducted can be mixed. The reaction will depend upon the rapport and interpersonal relationships established, as well as the degree of professional training displayed by the teacher. It is believed that teachers who are properly trained with appropriate resources, and who have well-defined objectives based on the interest and needs of the students, can do much to change the students' apprehension concerning teachers' competencies to instruct them in drug education.

All pupils need accurate information on which to base their decisions about drug use (Munro and Bellhouse 1999). This should include information about the law on drug abuse; the physiological and psychological effects of drugs; and a realistic account of their implications for the individual, the family, and wider society. They should be encouraged to reject drugs because they believe that it is the right thing to do and not just because they have been told to "Say no." Pupils need skills to help them resist pressure to experiment with drugs and they need positive attitudes toward living healthy lives that will be strong enough to influence their behavior. A more suitable approach is also needed where young people may have seen evidence in their local community of the profits associated with drug dealing and drug taking and where the lifestyle may therefore seem outwardly attractive (Martin, Duncan, and Zunich 1983; U.S. Department of Health and Human Services 1993).

Alongside direct teaching, there should be particular value in a more interactive approach to learning, including the use of audiovisual materials, role-playing, and group discussions. A number of organizations have developed imaginative and innovative materials and teaching approaches related to drug abuse, including video materials, mobile classrooms, puppetry, and theater in education groups.

A wide range of factual and educational resources is available at national and local levels to support drug education programs. This is a sensitive area of the curriculum and schools will need to judge for themselves which materials are appropriate for use with their pupils and best complement the approach to drug education that they intend to follow (Committee on Drug Abuse Prevention Research 1993).

SUMMARY

The need for collaborative planning in drug education is evident from research findings reported in this chapter. A coordinated approach is needed from all stakeholders in the community, including selected students. All aspects of the drug problem—legal, illegal, social, moral, medical, and psychological—should be incorporated into the drug program. Information and instruction should be given by individuals competent in their respective disciplines. A team-teaching model should be evident, with the teacher coordinating all instructional activities. Funding is essential for successful collaboration.

Financing drug education can consume a significant part of a school system's budget. There are private, state, and federal funds that might be consolidated. Data reflected throughout this chapter indicates that most of the drug programs supported by federal funds have not been justified. Drug Abuse Resistance Education (D.A.R.E.) is one of the major funded drug programs in this category. Along with funding for competent human resources, appropriate physical resources must also be considered.

REFERENCES

Aniskiewicz, R. E., and E. E. Wysong. 1987. *Project D.A.R.E. Evaluation Report*. Kokomo: Indian University at Kokomo, Department of Sociology.

Austin Independent School District. 1989. *Taking steps towards drug-free schools*. Austin, Tex.: Austin Independent School District. ED 313494.

Battjes, R. J. 1985. Prevention of adolescent drug abuse. *The International Journal of the Addictions* 20:1113–24.

Botvin, G. H. 1990. Substance abuse prevention: Theory, practice, and effectiveness. In *Drugs and Crime*, edited by M. Towery and J. Q. Wilson. Chicago, Ill.: University of Chicago Press.

Campo, A. T., and R. P. Rohner. 1992. Relationships between perceived parental acceptance-rejection, psychological adjustment, and substance abuse among young adults: Child abuse and neglect. *The International Journal* 16:429–40.

Committee on Drug Abuse Prevention Research, Commission on Behavioral and Social Sciences and Education. National Council, National Academy Press. 1993.

Dade County Public Schools. 1989. *A community education approach to substance abuse*. ED 311 341.

Dielman, T. E., D. D. Kloska, S. L. Leech, J. E. Schulenberg, and J. T. Shope. 1992. Susceptibility to peer pressure as an explanatory variable for the differential effectiveness of an alcohol misuse prevention program in elementary schools. *Journal of School Health* 62:233–37.

Dobkin, P.L., R. E. Tremblay, L. C. Masse, and F. Vitaro. 1995. Individual and peer characteristics in predicting boy's early onset of substance abuse: A seven-year longitudinal study. *Child Development* 66:1198–214.

Dusenbury, L., G. J. Botvin, and O. S. James. 1989. The primary prevention of adolescent substance abuse through the promotion of personal and social competence. *Prevention in Human Services* 7, no. 1:201–4.

Ennett, S. T., N. S. Tobler, C. L. Ringwalt, and R. L. Flewelling. 1994. How effective is drug abuse resistance education? A meta-analysis of project D.A.R.E. outcome evaluations. *American Journal of Public Health* 84:1394–401.

Fox, C. L., S. E. Forbing, and P. S. Anderson. 1988. A comprehensive approach to drug-free schools and communities. *Journal of School Health* 58, no. 9:365–69.

Glass, S. 1988. Truth and D.A.R.E.: The nation's most prestigious drug prevention program for kids is a failure. Why don't you know this? *Rolling Stone* (March 5): 42–43.

Goode, E., ed. 1991. *Annual editions: Drugs, society, and behavior 1991–1992.* Guilford, Conn.: Duskin Publishing.

Goodstadt, M. S. 1986. School-based drug education in North America: What is wrong? What can be done? *Journal of School Health* 56, no. 7:278–81.

Hansen, W. B., and R. B. McNeal. 1997. How D.A.R.E. works: An examination of program effects on mediating variables. *Health Education and Behavior* 24:165–76.

Johnston, L. D., P. M. O'Malley, and J. G. Bachman. 1996. *Monitoring the future survey: Summary of findings through 1995.* Ann Arbor: University of Michigan Press.

Kantor, G. K., B. D. Caudill, et al. 1992. Project impact: Teaching the teachers to intervene in student substance abuse problems. *Journal of Alcohol and Drug Education* 38, no. 1:11–29.

Klepp, K. I., A. Halper, and C. L. Perry. 1986. The efficacy of peer leaders in drug abuse prevention. *Journal of School Health* 56:407–11.

Komro, K. A., C. L. Perry, S. Veblen-Mortenson, and C. L. Williams. 1994. Peer participation in project northland: A community-wide alcohol use prevention project. *Journal of School Health* 64:318–22.

Law Enforcement News. 1996. When it comes to the young, antidrug efforts are going to pot. *Law Enforcement News* 22:441–47.

Martin, C. E., D. F. Duncan, and E. M. Zunich. 1983. Students' motives for discontinuing illicit drug taking. *Health Values: Achieving High Level Wellness* 7, no. 5:5–11.

McGovern, J. P., and R. L. DuPont. 1991. Student assistance programs: An important approach to drug abuse prevention. *Journal of School Health* 61:260–64.

Milgram, G. G. 1987. Alcohol and drug education programs. *Journal of Drug Education* 17:43–57.

Moore, D., and B. Saunders. 1991. Youth drug use and the prevention of problems. *The International Journal of Drug Policy* 2, no. 5:29–33.

Moore, D. D. 1993. New directions in prevention with at-risk students. *Journal of Emotional and Behavioral Problems* 2, no. 3:28–32.

Mothers against Misuse and Abuse. 1998. *Using alcohol responsibly.* Mosier, Ore.: Mothers against Misuse and Abuse.

———. 1999. *Drug consumer safety rules.* Mosier, Ore.: Mothers against Misuse and Abuse.

Mounts, N. S., and L. Steinberg. 1995. An ecological analysis of peer influence on adolescent grade point average and drug use. *Developmental Psychology* 31:915–22.

Munro, G., and R. Bellhouse. 1999. Next step: Educating young people about illegal drugs. *Center for Youth Drug Studies.* Melbourne: Australian Drug Foundation.

National Commission on Drug-Free Schools. 1990. *Toward a drug-free generation: A nation's responsibility.* Washington, D.C.: U.S. Department of Education.

National School Safety Center. 1988. *Drug traffic and abuse in schools.* NSSC Resource Paper. ED 307-530.

Nelson-Simley, K., and L. Erickson. 1995. The Nebraska network of drug-free youth program. *Journal of School Health* 65:49–53.

Office of National Drug Control Policy. 1997. *The national drug control strategy.* Washington, D.C.: Executive Office of the President. Document NCJ 163915.

Orlandi, M. A. 1986. Community-based substance abuse prevention: A multicultural perspective. *Journal of School Health* 56:394–401.

Palmer, J., and P. O. Paisley. 1991. Student assistance programs: A response to substance abuse. *School Counselor* 38:287–93.

Palmer, J., and C. L. Ringwalt. 1988. Prevalence of alcohol and drug use among North Carolina public school students. *Journal of School Health* 58:288–91.

Research Triangle Institute. 1994. *Past and future directions of DARE program: An evaluation review.* Research Triangle Park, N.C.: Research Triangle Institute.

Ringwalt, C. R., J. M. Greene, S. T. Salt, R. Iachan, and R. R. Clayton. 1994. *Past and future directions of the D.A.R.E. program: An evaluation review.* Final draft.

Rosenbaum, D. P., R. K. Flewelling, S. L. Bailey, C. L. Ringwalt, and D. L. Wilkinson. 1994. Cops in the classroom: A longitudinal evaluation of drug abuse resistance education. *Journal of Research in Crime and Delinquency* 31:3–31.

Silvia, E. S., and J. Thorne. 1997. School-based drug prevention programs: A longitudinal study in selected school districts. Research Triangle Park, N.C.: Research Triangle Institute, prepared for the U. S. Department of Education under contract LC9007001.

Stimmel, B. 1993. *The facts about drug use: Coping with drugs and alcohol in your family, at work, in your community.* New York: Haworth Medical Press.

Tobler, N. 1986. Beta-analysis of 143 adolescent drug prevention programs: Quantitative outcome results of program participants compared to a control or comparison group. *The Journal of Drug Issues* 16:537–67.

Tricker, R., and L. G. Davis. 1988. Implementing drug education in schools: An analysis of costs and teacher perceptions. *Journal of School Health* 58, no. 5:181–85.

U.S. Department of Education. 1990a. *Learning to live drug free: A curriculum model for prevention.* Rockville, Md.: National Clearinghouse for Alcohol and Drug Information, P.O. 2345.

———. 1990b. National goals for education. Washington, D.C.: U. S. Department of Education.

———. 2002. No Child Left Behind Act, at www.nochildleftbehind.gov (accessed 4 August 2003).

———. n.d. At www.ed.gov/offices/OESE/SDFS.

U.S. Department of Health and Human Services. 1993. *Young teens: Who they are and how to communicate with them about alcohol and other drugs.* Rockville, Md.: U.S. Department of Health and Human Services, Public Health Service, Substance Abuse and Mental Health Administration, Center for Substance Abuse Prevention.

Wolfe, B., and R. J. Meyers. 1999. Cost-effective alcohol treatment: The community reinforcement approach. *Cognitive and Behavioral Practice* 6, no. 2:105–9.

4

PARENTAL ROLES IN DETERRING SUBSTANCE ABUSE

Educators and counselors must discover innovative ways of involving parents and families in attempting to deter substance abuse among students (National Commission on Drug Free Schools 1991). Historically, this has not been the case. Generally, parents have not sought the school's aid in reducing drug usage by their children. Much of the noninvolvement has occurred because of hostility or parental indifference toward the school (Taylor 1997; Bickel 1995; Cohen and Linton 1995). Many educators consider some parents as nuisances, uneducated, lacking social graces, and not well informed on education and strategies for teaching children about the harmful effects of drugs. The relationship is further strained when parents internalize these negative behaviors displayed by the school and begin to view the school as a place where they are unaccepted (Skager 1999; Ertle 1995; Bickel 1995).

There must be a significant shift in the above paradigm if the drug problem, which is rampant in our schools, is to be addressed. Parental involvement is essential for any successful reduction in substance abuse.

Parents have the ability to stimulate their children in various ways concerning substance abuse:

1. They can introduce discussion concerning the harmful effects of taking drugs to their children at an early age, through conversations, videos, films, and other media .
2. They can create a safe, drug-free environment by establishing strict standards toward drug usage.
3. They can provide appropriate models concerning drug abuse and demonstrate appropriate role models for saying no to drugs. Practice makes perfect.
4. They can develop strong family ties, which in turn can develop and improve children's self-image, confidence, and attitudes. These traits begin at birth and are profoundly influenced by the family.
5. They can be sensitive to their children's signals. Sometimes fearfulness and negative behaviors, poor grades, or a lack of interest in school might be signs of drug problems.
6. They can keep in touch with drug initiatives by participating in PTA meetings.
7. They can express their attitudes and factual information relevant to drugs.
8. They can monitor their children's behaviors for signs of drug usage and assist them in developing constructive ways of managing stress.
9. They can serve as resource individuals in curriculum development.
10. They can note changes in the physical condition of their children, such as anger, attention span, mood changes, changes in speech patterns, withdrawal from family, and burns and bruises on the body, to name but a few.
11. They can communicate frequently with their children and inquire about their activities.
12. They can take pride in their children's achievements and praise them for their accomplishments.
13. They can monitor the types of friends their children associate with.
14. They can be familiar with the common street names of drugs.
15. They can assist their children in setting and achieving functional and realistic goals to govern their lives (Szapocnik 1995; National PTA 1996; Domino and Carroll 1994).

The aforementioned parental involvement strategies are in keeping with Goals 2000 (see appendix B) of the Educate America Act, which stated "By the year 2000, every school will promote partnerships that will increase parental involvement and participation in promoting the social, emotional, and academic growth of children."

A preponderance of research attests to the value of family involvement in educating children. Data supports the notion that children are more likely to be successful in the curriculum and show less-violent behaviors when unity exists in the family. Children also tend to report higher grades, not to be suspended or expelled from school, and not to take drugs if their parents have a high level of involvement in the schools. Additionally, research has shown that parental involvement is more important to children's success than other factors, such as family income or education.

The schools have not done an effective job in involving parents in the schools (Kelker 1990; Domino and Carroll 1994). Educators must embrace innovative ways of involving them, especially in drug education. Much of the fragmentation has occurred because of noninvolvement, hostility, or parental indifference toward the schools. Factors such as diversity in the school, both economic and cultural, combine to inhibit parental involvement in the schools. Diversity should be recognized as a strength rather than a weakness. Parents need to feel that their cultural styles and languages are valued knowledge that is needed and welcomed (Taylor 2000; Cross 1988; Harry, Allen, and McLaughlin 1995; Bickel 1995; Ertle 1995; Gardner, Green, and Marcus 1994; Allison and Leone 1994).

When diversity is considered along with community support, it can assist parents in understanding that they are part of creating and directing a drug education program, not simply being dictated to by the school.

EFFECTIVE PARENTING SKILLS

In order for parenting skills to be successful in teaching children about the harmful effects of substance abuse, parents need to be cognizant of the techniques and strategies to employ, which involve participation in school and community programs, reading literature on drug prevention, disciplining their children, and using effective community skills. Many parents do not have firsthand information related to drugs in their communities. They may have not been informed, may be new to the community, or might simply refuse to acknowledge that a drug problem exists and fail to react, hoping the drug problem will bypass their homes. It is, therefore, incumbent upon the school to provide information to parents and families about drugs in their communities (Bickel 1995; Cohen and Linton 1995).

In an effort to improve the behavior of their children, parents frequently apply too much pressure on them. This approach may lead many children to seek advice and comfort from their peers, which may be drug related. High standards and expectations should be jointly developed between parents and children. Some type of reward or reinforcement should be evident for conforming, thus reducing the amount of pressure applied by parents. When parents maintain a natural leadership in their homes, pressures on children are reduced because high expectations have been established. Additionally, natural leadership involves good communication, appropriate expectations, good problem-solving techniques, and listening to children's problems (Szapocnik 1995).

The importance of good parenting cannot be overlooked by the schools. Parents are the child's first teachers. The parental role in the family, therefore, focuses on being a role model for the child. Parents who express warmth, happiness, consideration, and respect in the handling of their children are acknowledged to be assisting the child in developing a positive approach to life. Parents need to have confidence that giving emotional support to their children will enable them to cope with the demands of family, friends, school, and peer pressure that might lead to drug usage (Winston 1994; Powell 1998; Gianneti and Sagarese 1999).

COMMUNICATION SKILLS

Communication is a skill that parents should perfect. Parents who communicate effectively with their children create a direct channel for closeness and the development of a positive self-concept that will be needed for later school success (Solo 1997; Taylor 1997; Anderson and Henry 1994). Communication skills of parents may be enhanced through building a sense of security and trust by maintaining a responsive home environment that is at-tuned with children's needs and desires. Parents also need to be aware of and sensitive to various signals given by their children that may indicate drug usage, such as changes in physical and psychological behaviors. Communication is also a form of sharing information and respecting diverse opinions. A home environment promoting and using positive communication skills will do much to combat and prevent drug usage among children.

PARENTAL REACTIONS

Parents show and display a variety of reactions when they discover that their children are using drugs. Some reactions are so severe that some parents will need psychological intervention to cope with the situation. Effective counseling techniques by competent counselors can do much to inform parents of the nature and extent of the problem. Parents need detailed information, explained in laymen's terms, about treatment, intervention and diagnostic evaluation, and community facilities and services relevant to treating substance abuse (McLaughlin and Vacha 1993). The age at which children begin to use drugs is of prime importance. The younger the child, the more effective preventive measures will be.

Parental involvement in drug prevention is most effective when it is comprehensively planned with the school and the community. Parents should be involved in developing drug curricula, assist in coordinating literature, serve as resource individuals, assist in coordinating school and community intervention strategies, and be a positive role model for their children. The school should provide in-service training to improve parental competencies in drug education and prevention. Attempting to prevent or educate children about the harmful effects of substance abuse is akin to trying to rake leaves in the opposite direction of a high wind. Many parents can serve as valuable resources and some may have expertise in drug education.

FAMILY–SCHOOL COLLABORATION

Children using drugs have a negative impact on the total family. Some spouses are unable to tolerate the behaviors displayed by their children using drugs. Siblings are also affected, who then may attempt to model the behaviors of their parents or siblings. Children may consume alcohol because they observe a parent drinking, or take drugs because they observe their mothers taking diet pills, or resort to selling drugs to reduce financial difficulties at home (Tharinger and Koranek 1988; Reese 1986; Stephenson, Henry, and Robinson 1996; Watkins and Durant 1996).

Additionally, research has shown that a family void of religious principles may result in depression and apathy on the part of children. Lack of a spiritual foundation may lead to negative, do-not-care attitudes, which might promote drug usage (Dobson 1990). Other researchers have voiced that parents have a significant impact on their children's decisions to use drugs. They may reduce this exposure by monitoring their children's activities, questioning strange behaviors, and noting the types of friendships they develop (Cohen and Linton 1995; Cohen and Rice 1995).

In support of this view, Jones (1977) articulated that an essential component of an effective drug program is parental and community involvement, and that all parents have information that can make the program successful. The school may tap this widely available source by encouraging family unity and support (Layne and Grossnickle 1989). Domino and Carroll (1994) wrote that this type of unity may satisfy the need of youths who otherwise might be driven to gang membership.

SUMMARY

Parental involvement is essential if the school is to successfully combat the drug problem. Parent–teacher conferences and meetings may be used to inform parents about drug usage. They may be introduced to various types of instructional materials and resources used, community resources, and information from specialists in the field. (Refer to appendix C for resources for parental involvement.)

Several researchers have attested to the value of parental involvement in the schools. Parents can engage in a variety of activities, some in the direction of the school and others independently (Bickel 1995; Cohen and Rice 1995; Ertle 1995; Szapocnik 1995). These authors have been comprehensive in recommending specific activities to improve parental involvement, and their recommendations are summarized as:

1. Parent volunteers identified by badges, can improve school safety by monitoring the campus, halls, and bathrooms. They can also sit in with teachers who are experiencing disruption in class.
2. Parent volunteers, can serve as "neighborhood watchers" to ensure students' safe travel to and from school, and to offer them protection from dealers and bullies.
3. Parents can work with schools and community groups to organize after-school and weekend programs to engage students constructively. They can also organize or chaperone proms, parties, and games that might be sites for drug activity.
4. Parents can initiate networks of parents to keep informed about local issues and to work together to keep their children safe. They can organize hotlines to keep others informed and to deal with crises. Parent mentors can provide parents new to the area with information about local drug prevention efforts and to encourage their involvement.
5. In groups, parents and children can share their thoughts and information about drug use so that local drug activity is revealed and parents' attitudes are clearly conveyed. Children can identify their friends so parents learn who might be influencing them.
6. Parents can institute family meetings, common in Latino households, that provide all members with a sense of belonging and provide an opportunity to discuss important issues and share concerns.

Information on the drug habits of children must be treated in a professional and confidential manner. Parents should be assured that information will be treated as a private matter. Technological advances and the information-explosion age have made confidentiality of information a major concern. Information electronically stored can easily be retrieved by individuals not associated with the prevention and treatment of children's substance abuse problems. Procedures should be in place to protect records.

REFERENCES

Allison, K., and P. E. Leone. 1994. The dual potentials model: Understanding alcohol and other drug use among ethnically and racially diverse adolescents.

In *Multicultural issues in the education of students with behavior disorders*, edited by R. L. Peterson and S. Ishii-Jordan, 63–77. Cambridge, Mass.: Brookline Brooks.

Anderson, A. R., and C. S. Henry. 1994. Family system characteristics and parental behaviors as predictors of adolescent substance abuse use. *Adolescence* 29:405–20.

Bickel, A. S. 1995. *Family involvement: Strategies for comprehensive alcohol, tobacco, and other drug use prevention programs.* Portland, Ore.: Western Center for Drug-Free Schools and Communities.

Cohen, D. A., and K. L. P. Linton. 1995. Parent participation in an adolescent drug abuse prevention program. *Journal of Drug Education* 25, no. 2:159–69.

Cohen, D. A., and J. C. Rice. 1995. A parent-targeted intervention for adolescent substance use prevention: Lessons learned. *Evaluation Review* 19, no. 2 (April): 159–80.

Cross, T. 1988. Services to minority populations: What does it mean to be a culturally competent professional? *Focal Point* 2, no. 4:1–3.

Dobson, J. 1990. *Children at risk.* Dallas, Tex.: Word Publishing.

Domino, V. A., and K. Carroll. 1994. Back to basics: Celebrating the family school-wide, curriculum-wide. *Schools in the Middle* 4, no. 2 (November): 13–17.

Ertle, V. 1995. *Sharing your success V: Summaries of successful programs and strategies supporting drug-free schools and communities.* Portland, Ore.: Northwest Regional Educational Laboratory and Western Center for Drug-Free Schools and Communities.

Gardner, S. E., P. F. Green, and C. M. Marcus, eds. 1994. *Signs of effectiveness II: Preventing alcohol, tobacco, and other drug use: A risk factor/resiliency-based approach.* Rockville, Md.: Center for Substance Abuse Prevention. ED 381 714.

Gianneti, C. C., and M. Sagarese. 1999. *Parenting 911: How to safeguard and rescue your 10- to 15-year-old from substance abuse, depression, sexual encounters, violence, failure in school, danger on the Internet, and other risky situations.* New York: Broadway Books. FAM 648.1 GIA B Family Book.

Harry, B., T. Allen, and M. McLaughlin. 1995. Communication versus compliance: African American parents involvement in special education. *Exceptional Children* 61, no. 4:364–77.

Jones, R. 1977. More than just no. *American School Board Journal* 184, no. 1 (January): 30–32.

Kelker, K. A. 1990. School services for drug-addicted children: What parents need to know. *Preventing School Failure* 34, no. 3:22–24.

Layne, D. J., and D. R. Grossnickle. 1989. A teamwork approach to the prevention of chemical abuse and dependency. *NASSP Bulletin* 73, no. 514:98–101.

McLaughlin, T. F., and E. F. Vacha. 1993. Substance abuse prevention in the schools: Roles for the school counselor. *Elementary School Guidance and Counseling* 28:124–32.

National Commission on Drug-Free Schools. 1990. *Toward a drug-free generation: A nation's responsibility.* Washington, D.C.: U.S. Department of Education.

National PTA. 1996. *Keeping youth drug-free: A guide for parents, grandparents, elders, mentors, and other caregivers.* Chicago, Ill.: National PTA. ED 398523.

Powell, D. R. 1998. Re-weaving parents into early childhood education programs. *Education Digest* 64, no. 3:22–25.

Reese, C., ed. 1986. Helping children from alcoholic families: Approaches and caregivers. *Children Today* 15, no. 1:13–16.

Skager, R. 1999. We're not the problem; it's the parents. *Prevention File*, no. 9:12.

Solo, L. 1997. School success begins at home. *Principal* 77 (2), 29–30.

Stephenson, A. L., C. S. Henry, and L. C. Robinson. 1996. Family characteristics and adolescent substance use. *Adolescence* 31:59–77.

Szapocnik, J., ed. 1995. A Hispanic/Latino family approach to substance abuse prevention. *CSAP Cultural Competence Series 2.* Rockville, Md.: Center for Substance Abuse Prevention. ED 400 489.

Taylor, G. R. 1997. *Curriculum strategies: Social skills intervention for young African American males.* Westport, Conn.: Praeger.

———. 2000. *Parental involvement: A practical guide for collaboration and teamwork for students with disabilities.* Springfield, Ill.: Charles C. Thomas.

Tharinger, D. J., and M. E. Koranek. 1988. Children of alcoholics—at risk and unserved: A review of research and service roles for school psychologists. *School Psychology Review* 17:166–91.

Watkins, K.P., and L. Durant Jr. 1996. *Working with children and families affected by substance abuse: A guide for early childhood education and human service staff.* West Nyack, N.Y.: Center for Applied Research in Education. 362.29130973 WAT-Book.

Winston, P. D. 1994. Families of children with disabilities. In *Exceptional children and youth*, edited by N. G. Haring, L. McCormick, and T. G. Haring. 6th ed. New York: Merrill.

5

SOCIAL INTERVENTION STRATEGIES IN REDUCING DRUG ABUSE

Several psychological factors are associated with drug abuse habits. These factors significantly affect the choice and effectiveness of treatments, which influences social development. Drugs have been found to have a severe impact upon the psychological development of many members of high-risk populations, as well as a significant portion of other populations. Drug-related psychological factors affect a wide range of relationships, including (1) parent–child interactions, where drugs influence positive communication between child and parent, (2) peer relationships influence drug-related behaviors and place high-risk populations at risk for experimenting with drugs, and (3) adult role models (like peer relations) influence how children react to drugs. Children frequently model the behaviors of adults they admire. Special social intervention strategies may be used to reduce, minimize, or eradicate the use of drugs that are rampant among high-risk minority populations (Taylor 1997).

One key to breaking the vicious drug cycle is the education of all youths (including these high-risk populations), directed toward the prevention of drug use and rehabilitation of drug users, with an emphasis on the causes and consequences of drug misuse and abuse. Social intervention should reflect the assessed social needs of the population. Several approaches may be used to reduce the use of drugs through the use of social intervention techniques.

McGinnis and Goldstein (1984) supported the concept of direct instruction of social skills, recommending modeling, role-playing, practice, and feedback as principal procedures and techniques to teach social skills. Additional instruction using the techniques discussed in this chapter can facilitate the teaching of social skills through direct instruction.

Direct instruction implies that the teacher is directly intervening to bring about a desired change. Direct instruction may be used with any subject area, including drug prevention and the harmful effects of drugs, to assist children in learning basic skills, as well as employing the concept of task analysis (step-by-step sequence of learning a task).

DIRECT INSTRUCTION FRAMEWORK

Bandura (1977) provided us with the conceptual framework for using direct instruction, advancing the concepts of social learning theory and behavioral modeling. He advocated that much of what we learn is through modeling from observing others. Information that is carefully and systematically gained through modeling may be transferred to other academic, social, and nonacademic functions, such as drug education. Specific techniques for using effective modeling and direct social skills training and interventions to reduce drug usage are delineated later in this chapter.

REDUCING DRUG ADDICTION THROUGH SOCIAL SKILLS INTERVENTION

The major theoretical premise underlying this approach is the belief that alcoholics have deficits in social graces and that this lack delimits the alcoholic's ability to deal appropriately with social issues within family, work, and interpersonal relationships. It is assumed that through the use of these social intervention models the desire for alcohol is reduced or controlled. Research finding by Channey, O'Leary, and Marlatt (1978) have not validated the effectiveness of social intervention in reducing drug abuse. A great deal of the lack of validation of social skills intervention may be attributed to alcoholics participating in other programs that may have had a social intervention component, such as the following programs.

Relapse Prevention

Channey, O'Leary, and Marlatt (1978) are among the major supporters of relapse prevention as a technique to be employed in treating alcoholism. A behavioral approach is used to reduce the causes that are viewed as precipitants in the relapse to alcohol and drugs. Other researchers support Marlatt's view in that they agree that reduced consumption is seen as the measure for positive behavioral changes (Miller, Hedrick, and Taylor 1983; Taylor 1993; Miller and Chappel 1991).

Brief Intervention

This strategy is premised upon the patient and the therapist reaching an understanding relevant to an agreed goal concerning the patient's drinking habit, based upon an agreed standard. The process is designed to assist the patient in reducing his or her drinking. Patients are expected to be realistic in selecting goals. Records are kept by the therapist and frequently reviewed with the patient.

Stress Management

Stress management is frequently combined with other forms of treatment such as aversion therapy (Blake 1967; Sission 1981). Aversion therapy is designed to produce an aversive reaction to alcohol by establishing a conditional response in an individual (Boland, Mellor, and Revasky 1978; Jackson and Smith 1978; Glover and McCue 1977). The ingestion of alcohol is paired with a negative stimulus in order to produce automatic negative responses, such as nausea, apnea, electric shock, and imagery, when the patient is exposed to alcohol.

The above social intervention techniques are frequently administered by trained therapists. Many states require that the therapists be licensed to treat patients using some of the above strategies. Generally, teachers are not trained to use these techniques in drug education programs. Social intervention techniques such as behavioral and cognitive approaches are most often used by teachers and educators in the classroom. These techniques are equally important in treating drug addiction.

OPERANT AND BEHAVIOR MODIFICATION TECHNIQUES

Behavioral modification techniques provide the teacher or counselor with strategies for assisting high-risk populations in performing desirable and appropriate behaviors, as well as promoting socially acceptable behaviors. It is a method to modify behavior to the extent that when a behavior is evinced in a variety of situations, it becomes consistently more appropriate.

Some cautions have been mentioned for teachers and counselors using behavioral strategies. The chief purpose of using this technique is to change or modify drug behaviors. The teacher or counselor is not generally concerned with the cause of the behaviors, rather with observing and recording overt behaviors. These behavioral responses can be measured and quantified in any attempt to explain behaviors. There are occasions, however, when motivation and the dynamic causes of the behaviors are primary concerns for the teacher or counselor.

In spite of the cautions involving the use of behavioral modification techniques, most of the research supports its use (Salend and Whittaker 1992; Lane and McWhirter 1992; Rizzo and Zabel 1988; Taylor 1992). The major concerns voiced were that the technique must be systematically employed; the environmental constraints must be considered; and teachers, educators, counselors, and parents must be well versed in using the technique. This is especially true when used with drug addicts.

Behavior can be modified in many ways. Contingency contracting, peer mediation, task-centered approaches, coaching, cueing, social-cognitive approaches, modeling, role-playing, cooperative learning, special group activities, skillstreaming, and cognitive behavior modification are to name but a few techniques to employ in reducing the drug intake of high-risk populations.

Contingency Contracting

This technique involves pupils in planning and executing contracts. Gradually, pupils take over record keeping, analyze their own behavior, and even suggest the timing for cessation of contracts. Microcontracts are made with the pupil, in which he or she agrees to execute some amount of low-probability behavior (Premack's principle) for a specified time. An example could be that an individual who likes to play sports will be denied the opportunity to play until homework assignments have been completed.

Peer Mediation Strategies

Peer mediation strategies have been successfully employed to manage drug behavior. The model is student driven and enables students to make decisions about issues and conflicts that have an impact upon their lives. The model requires that students exercise self-regulation strategies, which involves generating socially appropriate behavior in the absence of external control imposed by teachers or other authorities. To be effective, the concept must be practiced and frequently reinforced through role models and demonstrations of prosocial skills. A significant amount of drug usage may be attributed to peer pressure. This strategy promotes modeling appropriate behavior and denounces the use of drugs.

Several investigations have shown that negative behaviors and discipline problems decrease when this strategy is used. For example, an increase in cooperative relationships and academic advisement often follows. Findings also show an increase in task behaviors (Salend and Whittaker 1992; Lane and McWhirter 1992). Using this strategy with users, particularly young African American males, can assist them in internalizing appropriate behaviors by refusing to be influenced to take drugs.

Task-Centered Approach

The task-centered approach to learning is another way to modify drug behavior. Pupils may be experiencing difficulty because they cannot grasp certain social skills concepts. Behavioral problems may stem from the frustration of repeated failure, such as poor attention or the inability to work independently or in groups. This system provides children a highly structured learning environment. Elements in the task-centered approach may include activities to promote:

1. Attention-level tasks designed to gain and hold the pupil's attention.
2. Development of visual and auditory discrimination activities as needed.

3. Interpretation and reaction to social-level tasks emphasizing skills related to social interaction.
4. Imitation of social exchanges, the development of verbal and social courtesies, and group participation activities.

Coaching

Appropriate coaching techniques may be employed by teachers and counselors to develop social skills for high-risk populations using drugs. Some of the commonly known techniques include (1) participation, (2) paying attention, (3) cooperation, (4) taking turns, (5) sharing, (6) communication, and (7) offering assistance and encouragement. These techniques are designed to make individuals cognizant of using alternative methods to solving drug problems, anticipating the consequences of their behaviors, and developing plans for successfully coping with problems.

Cueing

Cueing is employed to remind students to act appropriately just before the correct action is expected rather than after an action is performed incorrectly. This technique is an excellent way of reminding students about prior standards and instruction. A major advantage is that it can be employed anywhere, using a variety of techniques such as glances, hand signals, pointing, nodding, shaking the head, or holding up the hand, to name but a few. Cueing can be utilized without interrupting the instructional program or planned activities. The technique assists in reducing negative practices and prevents students from performing inappropriate behaviors, including taking drugs.

Successful implementation of this technique requires that students thoroughly understand the requirement, as well as recognize the specific cue. Otherwise, the result might be confused students, especially when they are held accountable for not responding appropriately to the intended cue (Taylor 1997).

SOCIAL-COGNITIVE APPROACHES

These techniques are designed to instruct students and to help students maintain better control over their behaviors, and to deal more effectively with social and drug matters through self-correction and problem solving. Self-monitoring or instruction involves verbal prompting by the student concerning his or her social behavior. Verbal prompting may be overt or covert.

Making Better Choices

This social-cognitive approach is designed to assist high-risk students in making better choices when considering taking drugs. Group lessons are developed around improving social skills. Specifically, lessons promote forethought before engaging in a behavior and examining the consequences of the behavior. The major components of this program include the following cognitive sequence:

1. Stop (inhibit response)
2. Plan (behaviors leading to positive behaviors)
3. Do (follow plan and monitor behavior)
4. Check (evaluate the success of the plan)

These steps are practiced by the students and reinforced by the teacher and counselor. The teacher identifies various social skills for the student to practice. Progress reports are kept and assessed periodically by both teachers and students.

Modeling

Modeling assumes that an individual will imitate the behaviors displayed by others. The process is considered important because children acquire social skills through replicating behaviors demonstrated by others. Educators and adults may employ modeling techniques to influence drug behaviors by demonstrating appropriate skills to model. Teachers often overlook the impact and importance of this valuable technique and frequently fail to assess the impact of their own behaviors on children (Taylor 1998).

Modeling, if used appropriately, may influence or change behaviors more effectively than demonstrations of behavior. Consequently, many high-risk populations model drug behaviors they observe in their communities. This is premised upon the fact that once a behavior pattern is learned through imitation, it is maintained without employing positive reinforcement techniques. Teachers should be apprised and cognizant of the importance of modeling for promoting appropriate social skills. Additionally, they should be trained and exposed to various techniques to facilitate the process.

Children do not automatically imitate the models they see. Several factors are involved: (1) establishing rapport between teachers and children, (2) reinforcing consequences for demonstrating or not demonstrating the modeled behavior, and (3) determining the appropriate setting for modeling certain behaviors (Bandura and Walters 1963).

Students should be taught how to show or demonstrate positive behaviors by observing others performing positive behaviors in structured situations. The techniques provide for the structured learning of appropriate behaviors through examples and demonstration by others. Internal or incidental modeling may occur at any time, and modeling activities may be infused throughout the curriculum at random. However, a regular structured time or period of day is recommended in order to develop structure in a variety of social conditions. Teaching behavioral skills through modeling is best accomplished by beginning with impersonal situations similar to those that most students encounter, such as the correct way to show respect for others. Activities should be planned based upon the assessed needs of the class and be flexible enough to allow for changes when situations dictate. As students master the modeling process, additional behavioral problems may be emphasized (Taylor 1997).

Videotape Modeling

Videotape modeling is an effective way to improve self-concept. Children may be encouraged to analyze classroom behavior and the behaviors of addicts and patterns of interaction through reviewing videotapes. In this way, children can see the expected behaviors before they are exposed to them in various settings. Videotape modeling affords teachers the opportunity to reproduce the natural conditions of any behavior in the classroom setting. Consequently, videotape modeling may provide realistic training that can be transferred to real experiences inside and outside of the classroom.

For high-risk populations, educators may employ this technique to help transfer modeling skills to real-life situations. It has been proven an effective tool to teach prosocial skills to this group.

Role-Playing

Role-playing is an excellent technique for allowing children to act out both appropriate and inappropriate drug behaviors without embarrassment or without experiencing the consequences of their actions. It permits students to experience hypothetical conditions that may cause anxiety or emotional responses in ways that may enable them to better understand themselves. Once entrenched, these activities may be transferred to real-life experiences.

Role-playing may assist students in learning appropriate social skills through developing appropriate models by observing and discussing alternative behavioral approaches. Role-playing may be conducted in any type of classroom structure, level, or group size. It may be individually or group induced. Through appropriate observations and assessment procedures, areas of intervention may be identified for role-playing activities.

Role-playing assists children in identifying and solving problems within a group context. It is also beneficial to shy students. It encourages their interactions with classmates without adverse consequences. As with most group activities, role-playing must be structured. Activities should be designed to reduce, minimize, correct, or eliminate identified areas of deficits through the assessment process.

Gill (1991) listed the following advantages of role-playing:

- Allows the student to express hidden feelings.
- Is student-centered and addresses the needs and concerns of the student.
- Permits the group to control the content and pace.
- Enables the student to empathize with others and understand their problems.
- Portrays generalized social problems and dynamics of group interaction, formal and informal.
- Gives more reality and immediacy to academic descriptive material (history, geography, social skills, English).

- Enables the student to discuss private issues and problems.
- Provides an opportunity for inarticulate students and emphasizes the importance of nonverbal and emotional responses.
- Gives practice in various types of behavior.

Disadvantages include:

- The teacher can lose control over what is learned and the order in which it is learned.
- Simplifications can mislead.
- It may dominate the learning experiences to the exclusion of solid theory and facts.
- It is dependent upon the personality, quality, and mix of the teacher and students.
- It may be seen as too entertaining and frivolous.

Gill (1991) investigated the effects of role-play, modeling, and videotape playback on the self-concept of elementary school children, 13 percent of whom were African Americans. The Piers-Harris Children's Self-Concept Scale was employed on a pre-post-test basis. Intervention was for a six-month period. Data showed that the combination of role-playing, modeling, and videotape playback had some effect upon various dimensions of self-concept.

Cooperative Learning

A basic definition of cooperative learning is "learning through the use of groups." Five basic elements of cooperative learning are:

- Positive interdependence
- Individual accountability
- Group processing
- Small group/social skills
- Face-to-face interaction

A cooperative drug-education group is one in which two or more students work together toward a common goal in which every member of the group is included. Learning together in small groups has proven to

provide a sense of responsibility and an understanding of the importance of cooperation among youngsters (Adams 1990; Schultz 1990).
Children need to socialize and interact with each other. Among the best-
known cooperative structures are jigsaw classrooms, Student Teams
Achievement Divisions (STAD), think-pair-share techniques, group in-
vestigation, circle of learning, and simple structures.

Cooperative learning strategies have the power to expose youth to the
harmful effects of drug abuse. Harnessing and directing the power of
cooperative learning strategies in drug education presents a challenge to
the classroom teacher. Decisions about the content of the structure and
the current social skill development of the learners must be carefully
considered. For successful outcomes with students, teachers also need
follow-up peer coaches, administrative support, parent understanding,
and time to adapt to the strategies (Slavin 1991).

Cooperative learning practices in drug education vary tremendously.
The models can vary from complex to simple. Whatever their design,
cooperative strategies include:

- A common goal
- A structured task
- A structured team
- Clear roles
- Designated time frame
- Individual accountability
- A structured process

We need cooperative structures in our classrooms because many tradi-
tional socialization practices are absent. Not all students come to school
with a social orientation, and students appear to master content more ef-
ficiently within these structures (Kagan 1989b). The preponderance of research indicates that cooperative learning strategies motivate students to
care about each other and to share responsibility in completing tasks.

Special Group Activities

In a paper presented at the annual meeting of the American Education Research Association, Dorr-Bremme (1992) advanced some unique
techniques for improving social identity in kindergarten and first grade.

Students sat in groups and planned daily activities; these activities were videotaped. Analysis of the videotapes revealed several dimensions of social identity to be important, such as academic capability, maturity, talkativeness, independence, aggressiveness, ability to follow through, and leadership ability. The teacher responded to students individually and as circle participants, depending upon how the behavior was viewed.

Findings indicated that social identity was the combined responsibility of everyone in the classroom interacting to bring about the most positive social behavior. Interactions between individual students and the teacher were minimized.

Skillstreaming

Skillstreaming is a comprehensive social skills program developed by McGinnis and Goldstein (1984). Social skills are clustered in several categories with specific skills to be demonstrated to foster those human interaction skills needed to perform appropriate social acts. Clear directions are provided for forming the skillstreaming groups, conducting group meetings, and specifying rules. Activities include modeling, roleplaying, feedback, and transfer training. Feedback received in the form of praise, encouragement, and constructive criticism is designed to reinforce correct performance of the skills.

Cognitive Behavior Modification

These techniques focus on having individuals think about and internalize their feelings and behaviors before reacting. The process involves learning responses from the environment by listening, observing, and imitating others. Both cognition and language processes are mediated in solving problems and developing patterns of behaviors.

Cognitive behavioral strategies are designed to increase self-control of behavior through self-monitoring, self-evaluation, and self-reinforcement. The strategies assist children in internalizing their behaviors, comparing their behaviors against predetermined standards, and providing positive and negative feedback to themselves. Research findings indicate a positive relationship between what individuals think about themselves and the types of behaviors they display (Rizzo and Zabel

1988). This premise appears to be true for high-risk children as well. Matching the cognitive and affective process in designing learning experiences for the individual appears to be realistic and achievable within the school.

THE ROLE OF THE SCHOOL IN A BEHAVIORAL SETTING

A meaningful approach to dealing with drug abuse behaviors would be to isolate the behavior and then quantify, record, and observe the number of acts involved. When this determination has been made, the teacher or counselor is equipped to undertake a course of action to change the negative behavior. Social skills training is the technique advocated.

Children enter school with a wide range of learning abilities, interests, motivation, personality, attitudes, cultural orientations, and socioeconomic status. These traits and abilities must be recognized and incorporated into the instructional program (Bankee and Obiakor 1992).

Pupils also enter school with set behavioral styles. Frequently, these styles are inappropriate for the school. Several techniques are recommended to change inappropriate behaviors in the classroom:

- *Raise the tolerance of the teacher.* Teachers generally expect pupils to perform up to acceptable standards. Additionally, they often assume that pupils have been taught appropriate social skills at home. Whereas this may be true for most pupils, frequently it is not true for high-risk children. By recognizing causal factors, such as environment, culture, and values, the teacher's tolerance level may be raised.
- *Change teacher expectations for pupils.* Pupils generally live up to teacher's expectations. Teachers should expect positive behaviors from children. To accomplish this goal, behaviors will sometimes have to be modeled. It is also recommended that individual time be allowed for certain pupils through interviews and individual conferences where the teacher honestly relates how the child's behavior is objectionable.
- *Analyze teacher's behavior toward a pupil.* Pupils use teacher's overt behavior as a mirror of their strength in the classroom. When

a positive reflection is projected, the achievement level is increased. When the message is overtly negative, the pupil has nothing to support his or her efforts. For example, if there is little positive interaction between the pupil and teacher, the pupil may conclude that his or her behavior is not approved by the teacher. Because the pupil depends so heavily on the teacher's behavior for clues, it is crucial that the teacher objectively analyze his or her interaction with the pupils.

SUMMARY

Research findings have shown that high-risk students of lower socioeconomic status are significantly more likely to be involved in drug crimes than other groups of students.

Drug abuse by high-risk students who are poor, unemployed, and young is often to be found in the inner cities, ghettos, and slums. These youth tend to be singled out for especially stern punishment. The following recommendations have been made by Mauer and Huling (1995) to reverse this trend: (1) revise national drug spending priorities to offer treatment to the one million addicts who do not have access to treatment each year, (2) divert nonviolent property offenders and minor drug offenders to alternatives to incarceration, and (3) eliminate mandatory sentencing and other sentencing policies that have had a disproportionate impact on women and minorities.

Additionally, the available pool of minority teachers is declining. This is unfortunate because the literature has shown that high-risk students especially males, are in desperate need of role models. Without these models, individuals from high-risk environments may emulate inappropriate models to which they have been exposed, which frequently include forms of drug abuse. A significant amount of drug abuse is learned operant behavior; when positive models are introduced, drug behaviors are significantly reduced (Taylor 1997; Rosenberg 1979; Smart 1974; Miller and Hedrick 1983; O'Farrell and Feehan 1999).

Operant and behavioral models are designed to correct maladaptive behaviors. In the case of the drug addict, maladaptive social behaviors may be caused by the overusage of drugs. Strategies outlined in the model are designed to change behavior through introducing reinforcement for limiting the intake of drugs. A variety of approaches are used in behavioral intervention. Research findings have validated the use of these techniques to change maladaptive behavior in most social situations.

REFERENCES

Adams, D. N. 1990. Involving students in cooperative learning. *Teaching PreK–8* 20:51–52.

Bandura, A. 1977. *A social learning theory*. Englewood Cliffs, N.J.: Prentice Hall.

Bandura, A., and R. Walters. 1963. *Social learning and personality development*. New York: Rinehart and Winston.

Bankee, N. C., and F. E. Obiakor. 1992. Educating the black male: Renewed imperatives for black and white communities. *The Journal of Society of Educators and Scholars* 15, no. 2:16–31.

Blake, B. G. 1967. A follow up of alcoholic treated by behavior therapy. *Behavior Research and Theory* 5:89–94.

Boland, F. J., C. S. Mellor, and S. Revasky. 1978. Chemical aversion treatment of alcoholism: Lithium as the aversive agent. *Behavior Research and Therapy* 16:401–9.

Channey, E. F., M. R. O'Leary, and G. A. Marlatt. 1978. Skill training with alcoholic. *Journal of Consulting and Clinical Psychology* 45:1092–104.

Dorr-Bremme, D. W. 1992. *Discourse and social identity in a kindergarten-first grade classroom*. ERIC No. 352 111.

Gill, W. 1991. Jewish day schools and African-American youth. *Journal of Negro Education* 60, no. 4:566–80.

Glover, J. H., and P. A. McCue. 1977. Electrical aversion therapy with alcoholics: A comparative follow-up study: *British Journal of Psychiatry* 130:279–86.

Jackson, T. R., and J. W. Smith. 1978. A comparison of two aversion treatment methods of alcoholism. *Journal of Studies on Alcohol* 39:187–91.

Kagan, S. L. 1989. Early care and education: Beyond the schoolhouse doors. *Phi Delta Kappa* 71, no. 2:107–12.

Lane, P. S., and J. J. McWhirter. 1992. A peer mediation model: Conflict resolution for elementary and middle school children. *Elementary School Guidance and Counseling* 27:15–21.

Mauer, M., and T. Huling. 1995. Young black Americans and the criminal justice system: Five years later. *The Sentencing Project*. Washington, D.C.: U.S. Department of Justice.

McGinnis, E., and A. Goldstein. 1984. *Skillstreaming the elementary child*. Chicago, Ill.: Research Press Company.

Miller, N. S., and J. Chappel. 1991. History of disease concept. *Psychiatric Annals* 21, no. 12:1–8.

Miller, W. R., K. A. Hedrick, and C. A. Taylor. 1983. Addictive behaviors and life problems before and after behavioral treatment of problem drinkers. *Addictive Behaviors* 8:403–12.

O'Farrell, T. J., and M. Feeham. 1999. Alcoholism treatment and the family. Do family and individual treatment for alcoholic adults have preventive effects for children? *Journal of Studies on Alcohol* 13:125–29.

Rizzo, J. V., and R. H. Zabel. 1988. Educating children and adolescents with behavioral disorders: An integrative approach. Boston, Mass.: Allyn and Bacon.

Rosenberg, S. D. 1979. *Relaxation training and a differential assessment of alcoholism*. Unpublished PhD diss., California School of Professional Psychological. San Diego, Calif. University Microfilms no. 8004362.

Salend, S. J., and C. R. Whittaker. 1992. Group evaluation: A collaborative peer-mediated behavior management system. *Exceptional Children* 59:203–9.

Schultz, J. L. 1990. Cooperative learning: The first year. *Educational Leadership* 47, no. 4:43–45.

Sission, R. W. 1981. *The effect of three relaxation procedures on tension reduction and subsequent drinking of inpatient alcoholics*. Unpublished PhD diss., Southern Illinois University at Carbondale. University Microfilm no. 8122668.

Slavin, R. E. 1991. *Using student team learning*. Baltimore, Md.: Johns Hopkins University, Center for Social Organization of Schools.

Smart, R. C. 1974. Employed alcoholics treated voluntarily and under constructive coercion: A follow-up study. *Quarterly Journal of Studies on Alcohol* 35:196–209.

Taylor, G. R. 1992. *Impact of social learning theory on educating deprived/minority children*. Clearinghouse for Teacher Education. ERIC No. ED 349260. Washington, D.C.

———. 1993. *Black male project*. Report submitted to Sinclair Lane Elementary School. Baltimore, Md.: George R. Taylor.

———. 1997. *Curriculum strategies: Social skills intervention for young African American males*. Springfield, Ill.: Charles C. Thomas.

———. 1998. *Curriculum strategies for teaching social skills to the disabled: Dealing with inappropriate behavior*. Springfield, Ill.: Charles C. Thomas.

GUIDELINES FOR DEVELOPING FUNCTIONAL DRUG EDUCATION PROGRAMS AND CURRICULA

The increased addiction to hard drugs among children and youths is alarming. The common consensus is that the school should provide leadership to decrease this present trend. In response to the increase in drug abuse, as well as to pressures from parents, the community, and local, state, and federal officials, school districts have rapidly developed drug education programs on all grade levels (Goode 1993). Intervention should start as early as prekindergarten because many children have been exposed to drugs by this time. It is felt that schools are the best providers of a quality drug education program because virtually all children are exposed to their influence. To be charged with such a task, educators will have to plan systematically and comprehensively to develop quality programs that will reflect the many physical, social, and psychological problems faced by potential drug users as well as abusers (Joint Committee 1992).

Realistic and specific guidelines that can assist administrators in developing quality drug education programs are necessary. These guidelines should be designed to address all aspects of the drug problem, including promoting social and emotional growth and learning related to drug abuse, as well as providing information to construct a comprehensive drug education program stressing student, parent, community, and specialist involvement (Ellickson, Bell, and McGuigan 1993; Keller and Dermatis 1999; U.S. General Accounting Office 1993).

The voluminous amount of literature on drug abuse and drug education contains few experimental studies attesting to the effectiveness of drug education programs. Most of the research presents information relative to the legal, moral, and psychological aspects of the prevention, culture, and causes of drug addiction (Chassin 1984; Shedler and Block 1990). These studies have validated the need to use results from longitudinal and experimental studies to develop comprehensive drug education programs.

Development of a comprehensive drug program is expensive. It was hoped that with the signing of the Comprehensive Drug Abuse Prevention and Control Act by President Nixon on October 27, 1970, that school districts would have ample funds to develop comprehensive drug programs. However, this drug control bill has done little to reduce drug usage, especially for youths, and the reasons for this are identified throughout this chapter.

The three popular programs currently in use were developed to reduce drug intake among youth. They are Drug Awareness and Resistance Education (D.A.R.E.), Here's Looking at You, and McGruff's Drug Prevention and Child Protection program. Studies have shown that there is no empirical evidence to show that D.A.R.E. programs, Looking at You, and the McGruff programs are effective in reducing drug abuse. These programs have not had any significant impact on drug reduction among youths because they are not attuned with today's youth (Brown and Horowitz 1993; Brown et al. 1995; Brown 1997; Brown, D'Emidio-Caston, and Pollard 1997). One innovative approach that I do endorse, however, is Youths Serving Youths in Drug Education (Y.S.Y.D.E.). This program involves youths in all phases of the program. Chapter 7 contains specific details of this program.

In order for drug education programs to be effective, they must recognize students' abilities to make decisions relative to drug education, such as to differentiate between use and abuse (Brown 1997; Taylor 1972). The curricula should be age specific, stressing student participation and the provision of science-based, objective educational materials. In addition, a realistic and functional drug education program must have community support and have an evaluation component to determine its effectiveness for youths (Caliguri 1992; Dusenburg, Lake, and Falco 1997; Peele 1987).

BASIC FACTORS TO CONSIDER IN A DRUG EDUCATION PROGRAM

Drug education programs involve several critical components, the first being to develop goals, objectives, and activities that emphasize people, not drugs. Second, since the schools reach a large population of youth, it is realistic to assume that a drug program should be taught in the schools by school personnel. Third, students need to be involved; let them discuss the subject. The drug program should include interactive strategies, such as individual and group discussions, tuned to the culture and lifestyles of students, rather than didactic teaching adapted to the development level of the children. Fourth, the program should provide alternatives; instead of teaching that drugs have not provided the better life, show students that drugs are not needed to attain success in life. Fifth, a drug education program must be varied, must include the entire community, and must also include opportunities for parents to reinforce drug information and concepts specific to the drug problem in the community (Beck 1988).

DEVELOPMENT OF GUIDELINES

Taylor (1972) developed some basic factors needed in a drug education program and proposes several guidelines. These guidelines are not exhaustive and should be considered as one of many approaches in developing quality drug education programs for youths.

1. Early Intervention

Drug education programs should begin at an early age. If the vicious drug cycle is to be checked, programs should begin early to orientate children about drugs and their potential effects. It is suggested that programs begin in kindergarten and extend through grade 12.

Recent D.A.R.E. programs have dealt mostly with the middle and senior high schools. Programs have extended downward to the elementary grades as well. During the developmental stages (early childhood, middle childhood, and adolescence), children's physical and social environments are molding customs, attitudes, opinions, and concepts. It would appear that this is an opportune time for the schools to capitalize on this learning opportunity.

An example of a drug education program that includes kindergarten through grade 12 might list the following indicators:

- Building self-esteem
- Respecting the rights of others
- Respecting individual differences
- Learning methods of productive decision making
- Learning information on the use and misuse of drugs
- Reviewing information on health issues
- Learning how to make sound lifestyle choices

These indicators should be used on all grade levels, with experiences that are developmentally suited for children and youths in various content areas. (See curriculum development in chapter 7.)

2. Student, Parent, and Community Involvement

Student, parent, and community needs must be considered if drug education programs are to effectively serve the students. Instruments should be designed to elicit student, parent, and community attitudes and support towards eliminating the use of drugs, the danger of drugs, developing a drug education program, and participating in the program. Results should be used to develop a drug program based on the needs of the students, parents, and community. Student, family, and community participation can yield positive results that can invigorate the program content (Delgado-Gatan 1991).

3. Objectives

Clearly defined objectives should be written before any in-service training for a drug education program is initiated. Objectives, to a large extent, will determine the program content. Objectives for in-service workshops should be broad enough to reflect changes in teachers' attitudes concerning various facets of drugs and drug abuse, improved interpersonal relationships with students through more sympathetic attitudes towards their problems, and the involvement of parents and community personnel.

Objectives should be clearly stated in measurable terms so that the effectiveness of the program can be empirically evaluated at the end of the project. Workshop objectives as well as input from students and the community can aid in developing realistic objectives for the instructional aspect of the program. The nature of the instructional objectives will greatly depend upon the population to be served and special problems within a particular school district. The manner of organization and presentation of textual materials, audiovisual aids, student activities, and testing materials should all emanate from the course objectives.

4. Teacher Education

Intensive teacher and related school personnel education is essential for any successful drug education program. This is deemed important if teachers are to respond appropriately to students' impromptu questions concerning drugs and drug abuse. Exaggerated horror stories claiming that a diet pill may lead to heart failure, sterility, or insanity will not impress those who have seen local pill-heads alive and healthy on the streets. Much of the drug information heard by children and youths is replete with myths, half-truths, old wives' tales, and gross misinformation regarding the effects of various kinds of drugs.

A realistic program for teachers should be developed. Workshops designed for one or two days cannot adequately cover the wide gamut of the drug problem and will leave little room for innovation. What is needed is an intensive program that extends a week or longer, as well as college-based instruction given for credits.

An interdisciplinary approach should be evident for in-service workshops and college-based instructional courses, with many specialists included to cover the wide spectrum of illegal, legal, moral, social, educational, physical, medical, and psychological factors inherent in the problem. A panel composed of a doctor, lawyer, school nurse, teacher, physical education instructor, clergyman, psychologist, and social worker should be available to answer questions that might arise.

5. Diversification

As stated, an instructional program for drug education should be based on clearly defined objectives, the needs of the students and community, and the availability of resources and qualified personnel. An instructional program must be as diversified as the causes that lead to drugs and drug abuse. A well-rounded program is needed to dispel many of the myths about drugs, to decrease motivations that lead to drugs, and to give valid information concerning the illegal, legal, social, moral, medical, and psychological consequences of taking and using drugs (Schinke, Botvin, and Orlandi 1991).

The general impact of an instructional program should be a preventive one to deter some pupils by giving them sufficient education and self-understanding concerning the act of drug usage, to encourage pupils already using drugs to realize their need for help, and to provide channels through which they can actively seek assistance (Newcomb and Bentler 1998; Ponton 1997).

It is evident that many students are already knowledgeable about the various effects of certain drugs, and it is in part because of this knowledge that various drugs have become attractive and popular. Consequently, youths' responses and suggestions should be sought and used (Brown 1997).

Students should be permitted to enter a drug education program on a noncompulsory (voluntary) basis. Small-group sessions with no more than fifteen students appear to be the most effective for maximum group participation. The sessions should depend upon the needs and interests of the group involved. Skills in communicating with youths are important; equally important are systems and schedules of evaluation of the programs' objectives (O'Connor and Saunders 1992; Weiner, Prichard, et al. 1993).

An instructional program for drug education should not be limited to one content area but should be placed where the most students will receive maximum benefits, even though more than one content area might be involved. The individual makeup of the school, personnel, and resources will largely determine the content area in which a drug education program should operate.

6. Interdisciplinary

An interdisciplinary approach is needed to meet the many physical, psychological, and social problems inherent in educating youths about drugs and drug abuse. Specialists in various fields should be invited to reinforce the teachers' messages. Specialists can also distinguish the differences between drug usage and abuse from their professional viewpoints and assist in changing attitudes towards drugs (Tucker, Jalie, Donovan, and Marlatt 1999; Higgins and Silverman 1999). It is important for teachers and students to recognize that most substances have abuse potential—salt, sugar, aspirin, and most medicines—and that practically all drugs can be a source of abuse if not taken under controlled conditions. Again, specialists in various fields can render their expertise. Specialists should be scheduled to visit the class on regular intervals, depending upon the age and interest of the group. Some of the specialists invited to speak might include physicians, pharmacists, lawyers, clergymen, psychologists, social workers, and mental health specialists from local, state, or federal departments. School administrators should seek experts with ability and experience in their disciplines, as well as individuals who have an ability to relate to youths.

7. Specialized Training

To facilitate the instructional process, teachers and other personnel responsible for drug education programs should have specialized training attuned to the needs and characteristics of the group.

At this point, it is assumed that the teachers chosen to participate in the instructional program have had intensive in-service training or college training in various aspects of drug education. If not, they should not be included in the program. The teacher is the key person in any instructional program. He or she must be able to mold student attitudes and beliefs and create a rapport that will elicit students' respect and support. Thus, it is of prime importance that experts in the field expose teachers to various viewpoints concerning the drug problem. Intensive teacher education is essential if teachers are to adequately respond to questions with assurance. Teachers need detailed information to sway youths from turning to drugs. Reactions to the presence of a teacher in the room where a drug education program is held can be mixed. This will greatly depend upon the rapport and interpersonal relationships established, as well as the degree of professional training displayed by the teacher.

It is believed that teachers properly trained with a prepared teacher's handbook that defines the tasks or the instructional method, as well as clearly defined objectives based on the needs and interests of the students, can do much to change the students' apprehension. It is incumbent upon teachers to see that youths in our communities receive factual information about drugs, both use and misuse, in a manner that the youths can relate to.

Some students will listen more readily to other students than to faculty members on topics dealing with drugs; therefore, whatever educational program is developed will be more effective and generate more student enthusiasm if it is organized with the aid of students. Although it is felt that young persons can contribute greatly to a drug education program, it is recommended that they, too—as well as all adults involved—receive intensive in-service training under the supervision of qualified personnel, be carefully chosen, and be given a complete medical examination before working with youths. It is also believed that they should work under the direct supervision of the teacher and together plan and instruct youngsters about drugs. One example of this approach is Youths Serving Youths in Drug Education Programs (Y.S.Y.D.E.).

8. Preliminary Surveys

In order to determine the instructional needs of a program, surveys should be conducted in school districts in an effort to determine something about their approach to drug education. An additional approach would be to survey the availability of materials and resources needed to effectively conduct a drug education program in a particular school district. Instructional materials should be adjusted to the needs and interests of the group involved in the program. The instructional classroom for the program should not be isolated or remote from the rest of the school. It should be located where it will not readily call attention to it-self. Groups should be small for maximum participation and discussions. Finally, visual aid equipment should be readily available.

9. Guidance Program Availability

There should be a well-defined guidance program to assist drug users as well as potential users. Guidance, to be most effective, is a continu-ous process that should be instituted along with a drug education pro-gram. It will need to include both process and content in order to de-crease potential drug use as well as inform youths about drugs. Again, the guidance approaches to drug education must be as diversified as the causes leading to drug abuse, depending on the needs of the youth. At times, many of the specialists listed in the instructional process might be called upon to render their services in support of the educational efforts of the teacher or the counselor.

Group experiences of all kinds are needed. Guidance should be geared to utilizing youth talents under group conditions as well as in-volving individual youths who have symptoms of drug usage. Guidance should comprise the total academic setting, including the typical student (the clean-cut student or athlete) as well as the atypical student (the hip-pie, for example, or the pseudo hippie) to be effective. Guidance should be offered during regular school hours as well as after school hours to meet the many needs of youth.

10. Evaluation

Evaluation of a drug education program should be an ongoing process based upon measurable objectives of the instructional process. A few of the drug education programs reported in the literature attempted to evaluate the effectiveness of a drug education program (Tobler and Stratton 1997; U.S. General Accounting Office 1990, 1992, 1993; Weiner, Prichard, et al. 1993). Students and community people were given questionnaires at the end of the program. There were no indica-tions that a precriterion test was administered to determine drug knowl-edge or attitudes toward drugs and drug abuse. The success of these programs in terms of helping young people combat the drug problem cannot be fully realized until some initial assessment is made before youths enter a drug education program. It is almost impossible to determine whether one program is more effective, acceptable, or efficient than another because of the lack of adequate evaluation procedures.

The evaluation procedure should match the program's objectives and, where the program is designed to make specific changes in youngsters, these changes should be the basis for evaluation. In order to determine the full impact of a drug education program, student, school, and community personnel attitudes and knowledge must be assessed. Some following factors seem noteworthy of mention:

- *Assess prior attitudes and knowledge of the drug problem.*
- *List the objectives of the program in measurable terms.* These should be based upon student, school, and community input.
- *List the methods of evaluation.* Such instruments as objective tests, checklists, rating scales, attitudinal scales, and questionnaires may be instituted. These instruments should be administered on a pre- and post-basis and directly associated with the program's objectives. Instruments used in evaluating drug education programs must reflect both objective results that have been standardized and subjective results that include attitudes and opinions.
- *Collect data.* Some systematic approach should be evident for recording data from instruments used and characteristics of the subjects involved in the program. Data collected should reflect the objectives of the program. Other types of data not germane to the objectives are useless for evaluating the program.

Thus, the end product of evaluation should be reflected in behavioral changes shown by the students; that is, what the student does after the program compared to what he did before he entered (see chapter 9 for a comprehensive evaluation model).

11. Curriculum Planning and Development

Curriculum planning and development should be the final goal of a drug education program. Results from the evaluation of an instructional program in drug education should be one of the principal components used in developing a drug education curriculum. This information should reflect needed changes or modifications. Information gained from the evaluation process should be based on empirical methods.

Equally important is input from students, teachers, subject matter specialists, experts in various fields, and the community. This chapter is not intended to develop procedures needed in planning a curriculum, but to point out a series of tasks that should be followed to implement a quality drug education program, the curriculum being the end product, with provisions for changes as needed. (Refer to chapter 7 for a proposed curriculum in drug education.)

SUMMARY

In summary, the need for a comprehensive drug education program in the schools is evident. Well-planned and carefully controlled programs are needed, as well as empirical research to shed more light on the drug problem from all aspects—legal, illegal, social, moral, medical, and psychological.

Such research must be conducted in relation to the traits and characteristics of youths in elementary, junior high school/middle school, and senior high school, with emphasis on prevention, intervention, and treatment. The major consideration should be the achievement of better insight into these problems. From this should come constructive and practical aids that will enable administrators and other concerned personnel working with the drug problem to plan systematically and comprehensively to reduce drug usage by students. The end product of comprehensive planning should reflect a functional curriculum based on the needs and interests of students.

The use of guidelines appears to be one avenue designed to provide a quality drug education program for our youth because services provided by the school not only affect their academic achievement but the complete socialization process as well. The highest quality of conditions and services should be made available to decrease this social menace called "drug abuse."

An attempt was made to outline one approach that appears to offer instruction on how an effective program in drug education can be developed.

The guidelines can be used to assess programs under way or to aid in implementing the development of new drug education programs. The listed guidelines may be employed by school districts to develop a comprehensive drug education program designed to improve the social skills of youths in our schools. These articulated guidelines have been employed in constructing the drug curriculum in chapter 7.

REFERENCES

Beck, J. 1988. One hundred years of just say no versus just say know: Reevaluating drug education goals for the coming century. *Evaluation Review* 22, no. 1:15–45.

Brown, J. H. 1997. Listen to the kids. *American School Board Journal* 184:38–47.

Brown, J. H., M. D'Emidio-Caston, and J. Pollard. 1997. Students and substances: Social power in drug education. *Educational Evaluation and Policy Analysis* 19:65–68.

Brown, J. H., and J. E. Horowitz. 1993. Deviance and deviants: Why adolescents substance use prevention programs do not work. *Evaluation Review* 17, no. 5:29–55.

Caliguri, J. P. 1992. Drug education in the schools: Does it have a future? *Journal of Alcohol and Drug Education* 37, no. 3:17–22.

Chassin, L. 1984. Adolescent substance use and abuse. *Advances in Child Behavioral Analysis and Therapy* 3:99–152.

Delgado-Gatan, C. 1991. Involving parents in the schools: A process of empowerment. *American Journal of Education* 100:20–46.

Dusenbury, L., A. Lake, and M. Falco. 1997. A review of the evaluation of 47 drug abuse prevention curricula available nationally. *Journal of School Health* 67, no. 4:127–32.

Ellickson, P. L., R. M. Bell, and K. McGuigan. 1993. Preventing adolescent drug use: Long-term results of a junior high program. *Journal of Public Health* 83, no. 6: 856–61.

Goode, E. 1993. *Drugs in American society*. New York: McGraw-Hill.

Higgins, S. T., and K. Silverman. 1999. *Motivating behavior change among illicit drug abuse: Research on contingency management interventions*. Washington, D.C.: American Psychological Association.

Joint Committee on the Association for the Advancement of Health Education and American School Health Association.1992. Health instruction responsibilities and competencies for elementary (K–6) classroom teachers. *Journal of School Health* 62, no. 2: 76–77.

Keller, D., and H. Dermatis. 1999. Current status of professional training in the addictions. *Substance Abuse* 20, no. 3:122–40.

Newcomb, M., and P. Bentler. 1988. *Consequences of adolescent drug use: Impact on the lives of young adults.* Newbury Park, Calif.: Sage.

O'Connor, J., and B. C. Saunders. 1992. Drug education: An appraisal of the popular preventive. *The International Journal of Addictions* 27, no. 2:165–85.

Peele, S. 1987. Running scared: We're too frightened to deal with the real issues in adolescent substance abuse. *Health Education Review* 2:423–32.

Ponton, L. 1997. *The romance of risk: Why do teenagers do the things they do?* New York: Basic Books.

Schinke, S., G. Botvin, and M. A. Orlandi. 1991. *Substance abuse in children and adolescents: Evaluation and intervention.* Newbury Park, Calif.: Sage.

Shedler, J., and J. Block. 1990. Adolescent drug use and psychological health: A longitudinal inquiry. *American Psychologist* 45:612–30.

Taylor, G. R. 1972. Toward a model K–12 program in drug education. *Association of California School Administrators* 1, no. 4:28–32.

Tobler, N. S., and H. H. Stratton. 1997. Effectiveness of school-based drug prevention programs: A meta-analysis of the research. *The Journal of Primary Prevention* 18, no. 1:71–128.

Tucker, J., A. Jalie, D. Donovan, and G. A. Marlatt. 1999. *Changing addictive behavior: Bridging clinical and public health strategies.* New York: Guildford Press.

U.S. General Accounting Office. 1990. *Drug education: School-based programs seen as useful but impact unknown.* Report to the Chairman, Committee on Governmental Affairs, U. S. Senate. Washington, D.C.: U.S. General Accounting Office.

———. 1992. *Adolescent drug use prevention: Common features of promising community programs.* Report to the Chairman, Subcommittee on Select Education, Committee on Labor. Washington, D.C.: U.S. General Accounting Office.

———. 1993. *Drug use among youth: No simple answers to guide prevention.* Washington, D.C.: U.S. General Accounting Office.

Weiner, R. L., C. Prichard, et al. 1993. Evaluation of drug-free schools and community programs. *Evaluation Review* 17, no. 5:488–503.

7

A MODEL DRUG CURRICULUM

Curriculum development is designed to reflect the course of study in schools. A drug curriculum is designed to reflect the course of study in drug education. Like any curriculum, a drug curriculum is intended to present information to students in an organized manner through various methods and instructional strategies. Drug curricula may be designed to address the following content areas:

- Social skills
- Decision making
- Personal management skills
- Risks and consequences
- Resisting pressure

The amount of time devoted to the content area will depend upon the needs and interests of the student and community. Educators must be cognizant of creative and innovative ways to maximize drug information for students (Hansen 1992; Bosworth and Sailes 1993).

A drug curriculum should be designed to:

1. Provide students with information on the use and misuse of drugs.

2. Inform students that all medicines are drugs but not all drugs are medicines.
3. Inform students that all drugs can be harmful if not used appropriately.
4. Provide information relative to the medical values of drugs.
5. Practice safe habits with household medications.
6. Inform students about the legal and illegal aspects of drugs.
7. Be assertive and exercise skills in resisting pressure from friends to take drugs.
8. Know the consequences of and reasons why people take drugs.
9. Prepare students to deal with frustrations and anxieties without taking drugs.
10. Apprise students of the importance and beneficial values of drugs.

NEEDS ASSESSMENT

The program should take into account the problems, culture, and norms of the community, which can only be determined by a needs assessment prior to implementing a specific curriculum (Fox, Forbing, and Anderson 1988). Surveys, essay tests, rating scales, checklists, questionnaires, and interviews are typical information-gathering methods (Taylor 2002). These may be supplemented with secondary sources of information, such as school absenteeism and dropout rates, drug-related hospital admission data, and arrest rates for drug use and drug-related crimes.

Focus groups in the community may be used to determine what they perceive the drug problems to be. Focus groups are beneficial for identifying of major categories and themes relevant to drug usage in the community. The assessor must be sensible to the culture and diversity of the groups. Focus groups can provide specific information and a wealth of data if properly conducted. They permit the assessor to dive into the real drug issues, perceptions, attitudes, and opinions of the participants. Consequently, focus groups can contribute significantly to drug programs as viewed by the community, as long as views of the group are carefully considered and well respected (Krueger 1994).

Once the drug education needs of the community have been determined, by using the aforementioned assessment strategies, they will have to be prioritized. There are usually more needs generated through the process than can be addressed by the drug curriculum. The team responsible for developing the curriculum should determine priorities.

Because a curriculum must reflect all of the experiences afforded, its content must be broad enough in scope to prepare students to meet their present as well as future needs. In order to achieve these goals, the following eight principles of curriculum are suggested:

1. A curriculum should have social validity; how well does the curriculum address the social skills needed by all learners to function successfully in society?
2. A curriculum should focus on integration; how well do all of the major components in a curriculum address the various developmental stages of the learners?
3. A curriculum should contain all required skills, as reflected in the goals and objectives, as well as those skills required to function successfully in the school and the community.
4. A curriculum should reflect the demands of both current and future environments; curricula should address skills needed for learners to react successfully in a variety of settings at different developmental stages.
5. A curriculum should have objectives and pathways broad enough to respond to the needs of all learners in the program; curriculum experiences should be based on realistic goals and objectives. These goals and objectives should take into consideration the needs, capacities, and interests of disabled learners as they interact with their environment. Diverse learning styles and other characteristics should be considered and curriculum experiences modified and adapted to the unique needs of each disabled learner.
6. A curriculum should serve as a referent for monitoring instruction; assessment data should enable educators to order and sequence tasks as well as change tasks when objectives are not being met.
7. A curriculum should be seen as a local responsibility and define the purpose of the instructional program because school districts are in the best place to assess the needs of all students, including disabled individuals, in their school districts. Additionally, local school districts can readily identify and coordinate the instructional program.

8. A curriculum should promote coordination, collaboration, and continuity across instructional programs; due to the complex problems of disabled learners in most areas of human functioning, services must be well coordinated.

These principles have relevance for developing drug curriculum. Many of the principles were listed by Bosworth and Sailes (1993) in developing content and teaching strategies in drug education. These principles are recommended for educators developing drug curricula.

PRINCIPLES OF CURRICULUM DEVELOPMENT

It is not within the scope of this book to develop a complete curriculum guide but rather to present concepts and strategies needed to develop one. Data in appendices D and E are designed to provide educators with examples of the resources and strategies used in developing instructional units from curricula. Keep in mind that curriculum development requires participation from many segments of our society, including local education agencies and specialists from various disciplines.

Coordination of services must be established between all agencies in the public and private sectors that provide services to youth. Planning curriculum experiences, if they are to be successful, must include collaboration with community agencies. Information should be presented by qualified professionals to promote the development of appropriate drug information.

Consultant services may be needed in various disciplines to assist in curriculum development. An integrated approach is needed, which may require the assistance and services of several specialists and be coordinated with the school (George 1996). Joint participation of school and allied disciplines enables research and current findings to be applied to develop a broad framework that may be adapted for developing curricula.

Designing a drug curriculum involves two major methodologies. The first methodology is experiential instruction. Experiential instruction is designed to intrinsically motivate student interest inside and outside of the classroom. The second approach is systematic instruction. Teacher–student interaction underlies this methodology. The major purpose of systematic instruction is to develop a skill in concept and develop materials and activities that enable students to achieve selected objectives. The following strategies are recommended to assist students in achieving the stated objectives.

Curriculum development in most school districts is concerned with developing academics in order to equip pupils to master the complex tasks in our society. This point of view is endorsed for most pupils, including the disabled, and examples are seat work, homework, games, lectures, media, small groups, brainstorming, role-playing, and discussions. The amount of time devoted to these strategies will depend upon the needs characteristics and interests of the children (Bosworth and Sailes 1993).

CURRICULUM DEVELOPMENT

Central to drug education is the provision of age-appropriate information about tobacco, alcohol, and other drugs; symptoms of drug use; factors associated with dependency; and legal aspects of drug use. In addition, and common to all areas of health education, the curriculum should offer activities (such as role-playing) for the development of peer refusal skills, self-esteem, assertiveness, and problem-solving skills. Curriculum options include purchasing a curriculum, developing the curriculum within each school, or a combination of both (Hansen 1992).

Tobacco, drug, and alcohol education also offer many opportunities to infuse content into other curricular areas. Language arts, science, math, health, social studies, and driver education are among classes in which various aspects of substance use might be incorporated (Dunkle and Nash 1991; Joint Committee on Health Education 1990; Joint Committee on the Association 1992).

The notion of "curriculum" may be broadened in a comprehensive drug and alcohol prevention program to include treatment referral for those who are substance-dependent and post-treatment aftercare for those returning to school. Some programs have found success with support groups, peer teachers, and peer counselors (Fox, Forbing, and Anderson 1988). A proposed approach to drug education is "Youths Serving Youths in Drug Education" (Y.S.Y.D.E.), mentioned earlier.

Research findings have clearly endorsed and recommended youth involvement in drug curricula (Black, Tobler, and Sciacca 1998; Lisnov, Harding, Safer, and Kavanagh 1998; Brown 1995, 1997). The name

"Youths Serving Youths in Drug Education" implies that youths should be directly involved in the development, construction, implementation, and evaluation of drug curricula. Data from the cited research indicates that youth input significantly increases abstinence. Research cited in chapters 2 and 8 has shown that many drug intervention programs have little effect on reducing drug usage. Additionally, many of the programs cited do not include youths to a significant degree. Youths are equipped to present factual information about the consequences of drug, alcohol, and nicotine addiction and to demonstrate the fallacy of youths' belief that drugs can alleviate their pain. Youths offer skill-building curricula that cover clear communication, anger management, conflict resolution, and self-esteem. Youth servers can communicate effectively with peers about drug matters (in some instances, better than educators and other professionals). Consequently, youth involvement appears to be essential in developing realistic, functional curricula based upon the unique needs and interest of youth. Youth involvement should be supervised by competent personnel. In my view, Y.S.Y.D.E. is the missing link to effective drug education programs.

CHARACTERISTIC OF CURRICULA

Curricula are written to assist youths to achieve broad goals as deemed important by society. Depending upon the type of subject matter, these broad curricula are written for at-risk youths who have common needs and traits or characteristics. Individualization of instruction is an attempt to adapt the broadly defined curricula to the unique needs and learning styles of at-risk youths. Characteristics of curricula differ based upon the abilities and disabilities, subject content, location of the facility, and the educational environment in which the instruction will be conducted (Denver and Knapczyk 1997).

According to Bigge (1998) and Shujaa (1995), an effective curriculum consists of all experiences offered the child in his or her logical environment and is based upon the development of the child and the culture of the society in which he or she lives. Cultural values significantly influence the nature and type of drug curriculum experiences reflected. In the case of many youths, curriculum experiences and development must reflect the immediate and long-range goals for the child correlated with his or her developmental sequence and functional levels. Thus, scope, objective, and sequence are essential factors in planning a drug curriculum.

Curriculum should be based upon skills needed in order for youths to function successfully in their society. Much of the research reviewed indicates that a significant number of youths are drug abusers.

A Functional Approach

A functional approach to teaching youth drug education can easily be infused throughout the curriculum. Such an approach involves exposing the learner to real-life situations and activities that he or she will experience in life. Each curricula area we have discussed emphasizes a practical and functional approach (Taylor 1998).

Several group activities under each of the curriculum domains reflect a functional and holistic viewpoint within the content of real-life experiences. In essence, youths should be taught to model, imitate, and demonstrate appropriate skills in the reality in which they exist. A creative curriculum that serves the individual needs of the learners is critical to their success.

The degree of variability among children becomes greater as they become older, thus, drug education should be provided at an early age and programmed in sequential steps throughout their school experiences. One of the major means of achieving the aforementioned is through developing curricula based upon achievable objectives. The curriculum should encompass all the planned experiences provided by the school to assist youths in attaining learning outcomes. It bridges the past, the present, and indicates future changes needed to prepare youths to become functional and contributing members of our society.

Curriculum planners for programs must anticipate the shifts and changes in society in order to make curriculum relevant to those changes. Curriculum experiences should be designed to meet the short- as well as long-range needs of youths at risk for taking drugs. In order to achieve this goal, I decided to demonstrate functional approaches and activities for developing curricula by using certain segments from each curriculum in developing instructional units.

Sequence in Curriculum

The initial step in developing a drug curriculum is to identify the scope of the proposed program. The scope refers to the breadth and width of the general drug behaviors to be changed. These behaviors should be written as general objectives, which should provide the framework for constructing activities. The involvement of youths is essential (Taylor 1999).

The second step is to sequence *specific* objectives as they relate to the goals and *overall* objectives. They should be studied in behavioral and measurable terms (Fox, Forbing, and Anderson 1988).

The third step is to identify activities and resources that will achieve the stated objectives through assessing the drug needs of the community and stakeholders. The activities should be agreed upon by all stakeholders and reflect ways in which drug abuse can be reduced or eliminated in the community. The Y.S.Y.D.E. concept should be endorsed (Black, Tobler, and Sciacca 1998).

The fourth step is to include cultural, ethnic, and racial diversity into the curriculum, as reflected in the community. Activities should include multicultural activities unique to the community. Youths' comments and suggestions should be sought (Botvin, Schinke, and Orlandi 1995).

Curriculum Format

There are several factors that educators may employ in developing curricula, depending upon the standards or strategies adopted by a school district. Any format developed should be logically sequenced from stating observable and measurable objectives to assessment and evaluation of progress. The format recommended by this book has been abstracted from several areas of the curriculum and instructional units commonly used to instruct youths at risk for taking drugs. Additionally, I provide a recommended format for educators to use. In my opinion, employing the use of a common format enables educators to become more competent and better able to carry out an effective instructional program. The format in table 7.1 is recommended.

Table 7.1. Description of the Lesson

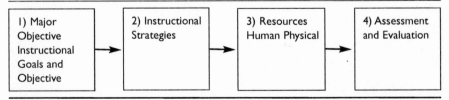

| 1) Major Objective Instructional Goals and Objective | 2) Instructional Strategies | 3) Resources Human Physical | 4) Assessment and Evaluation |

In each of the curricula areas addressed in this text, this common format, shown in table 7.1, should be used. Each instructional objective is achieved through using realistic and functional instructional strategies. Under instructional objectives, all objectives are sequenced; teachers model activities for students, who model activities themselves until mastery has been achieved. Students practice the skills independently. Both human and physical resources should be employed. The use of cultural diversity and learning styles under the human category, and computer technology under the physical category, are essential to the drug program. Strategies for assessing and evaluating each curriculum area are summarized. This format and set of strategies should be employed for all curriculum and instructional units discussed.

DRUG EDUCATION BY AGE LEVELS

A comprehensive drug education program should address all grade levels (K–12). Information for the various grade levels should be determined based upon the age, abilities, disabilities, development levels, and assessed needs of the students. For each grade level, unified curriculum strands should be identified, such as social skills, decision making, and strategies to resist drugs (Bosworth and Sailes 1993).

Recommended age level for curricula areas to be addressed in drug education are:

- Age Level 5–8   Should have content relevant to taking drugs as medicine; know that using or taking too much of household items may be harmful, know that parents or adults should supervise taking medical drugs, and know how to be assertive and resist peer pressure. Students in this age group are usually in grades K–3.

- Age Level 7–12   Should have content relevant to the harmful effects of taking drugs such as tobacco, alcohol, and other chemical substances. Students in this age group are usually in grades 4–7

(Kreutter, Gewirtz, Davenny, and Love 1991; Flannery and Torquati 1993).

- Age Level 12–15   Should know that substance abuse can affect one's health by lowering the body's natural defenses and damaging vital organs in the body, as well as affecting emotions, intelligence, and memory. They should know about HIV, AIDS, and STDs, and their relationship to drug abuse. Students in this age group are usually in grades 7, 8, 9, and 10.

- Age Level 16–18   Review and expand information concerning the harmful affects of drugs on the body, peer pressure, and decision-making skills concerning the use of drugs and ways to solve problems associated with drugs. This age group is comprised of senior high students in grades 11 and 12.

Educators developing drug curricula should make adjustments in the above strategies based upon the needs of the students and the community (Gingiss, Gottlieb, and Brink 1994). The levels are presented only as guidelines. Equally important, educators must decide upon the placement of a drug curriculum. Will it be a separate unit or integrated and infused with other disciplines? Most of the research outlined in this text supports integration and infusion (Diller and Glessner 1988).

EVALUATION OF A DRUG CURRICULUM

General evaluation techniques are outlined earlier in the chapter. Techniques will only be summarized at this point. If results are to be effectively used to gauge the extent to which the stated objectives have been achieved, then the evaluation process must be properly planned prior to employing procedures for assessing the skills of individuals (Hopkins, Mauss, Kearney, and Weisheit 1988). A decision must be made on what to evaluate. This approach facilitates the selection of appropriate drug methods and techniques, such as:

- Evaluating the competence of a particular skill
- Determining the baseline behavior for a particular skills
- Using results to revise the unit
- Providing information to gauge the drug knowledge of youths
- Appraising the effectiveness of selected skill activities
- Ensuring that youths at risk for taking drugs have the necessary prerequisites for performing the skills
- Having the necessary physical and human resources to conduct the unit
- Eliciting the cooperation of parents
- Providing training for parents to follow up at home
- Determining youths' reactions toward substance abuse

Program evaluation is often cursory and conducted as an afterthought. However, since program evaluation accountability may justify expenditures of money and time, a broad approach that examines knowledge, attitudes, and behaviors is appropriate. Some prepackaged curricula include evaluative tools. (Refer to chapter 9 for specific evaluation strategies.)

SUMMARY

The need for comprehensive drug education curricula in the school is evident from the voluminous amount of literature reported throughout this text and chapter. New approaches are needed as well as empirical research to shed additional information on the legal, illegal, social, moral, medical, and psychological aspects of drug usage. It has been emphasized throughout this chapter that effective drug curricula should be based on the types and characteristics of children served, with an emphasis on prevention, intervention, treatment, and a total involvement of youth. Equally important is the consideration of the needs of the community. The end product of comprehensive planning should reflect a functional drug curriculum that should not be passive (relying solely on pamphlets, lectures, films, and other similar methods of reaching the students and the community). The emphasis should be on actual data and activities that expose and demonstrate to youths the harmful effects of drugs.

The literature concerning the development of drug curricula abounds with recommended strategies and approaches. An attempt was made in this chapter to abstract models from these curricula and to propose strategies for making functional curricula. The uniqueness of the proposed model is that it is student centered. Students do a significant part of the planning and development of the curriculum under the supervision of competent stakeholders. The term for this innovative approach is Youths Serving Youths in Drug Education (Y.S.Y.D.E.). Many attempts to reduce drug usage have failed because the involvement of youths was not considered essential to the success of the programs. It is hoped that school districts and community agencies responsible for developing drug curricula will recognize and utilize this valuable resource to the fullest.

REFERENCES

Bigge, J. 1988. *Curriculum-based instruction for special education students*. Mountain View, Calif.: Mayfield.

Black, D. R., N. S. Tobler, and J. P. Sciacca. 1998. Peer helping/involvement: An efficacious way to meet the challenge of reducing alcohol, tobacco, and other drug use among youth? *Journal of School Health* 68:87–93.

Bosworth, K., and J. Sailes. 1993. Content and teaching strategies in ten selected drug abuse prevention curricula. *Journal of School Health* 63:247–53.

Botvin, G. J., S. Schinke, and M. A. Orlandi, eds. 1995. *Drug abuse prevention with multiethnic youth*. Thousand Oaks, Calif.: Sage.

Brown, J. H. 1995. *Tuning out and turning on: Student response to contemporary drug education*. New York: Lindesmith Center. Audiotape of seminar presentation.

———. 1997. Listen to the kids. *American School Board Journal* 184, no. 12:38–40.

Dever, R. B., and D. R. Knapczyk. 1997. *Teaching persons with mental retardation: A model for curriculum development and teaching*. Madison, Wis.: Brown and Benchmark.

Diller, C., and B. Glessner. 1988. A cross curriculum substance abuse unit. *Journal of Reading* 31:553–58.

Dunkle, M. C., and M. A. Nash, eds. 1991. *Beyond the health room*. Washington, D.C.: Council of Chief State School Officers.

Flannery, D. J., and J. Torquati. 1993. An elementary school substance abuse prevention program: Teacher and administrator perspectives. *Journal of Drug Education* 23, no. 4:387–97.

Fox, C. L., S. E. Forbing, and P. S. Anderson. 1988. A comprehensive approach to drug-free schools and communities. *Journal of School Health* 58, no. 9:365–69.

George, P. S. 1996. Arguing integrated curriculum. *Education Digest* 62, no. 96:16–21.

Gingiss, P. L., N. H. Gottlieb, and S. G. Brink. 1994. Increasing teacher receptivity toward use of tobacco prevention education programs. *Journal of Drug Education* 24, no. 2:163–76.

Hansen, W. B. 1992. School-based substance abuse prevention: A review of the state of the art in curriculum, 1980–1990. *Health Education Review* 7, no. 3:403–30.

Hopkins, R. H., A. L. Mauss, K. A. Kearney, and R. A. Weisheit. 1988. Comprehensive evaluation of a model alcohol education curriculum. *Journal of Studies on Alcohol* 49, no. 38:50–55.

Joint Committee on the Association for the Advancement of Health Education and American School Health Association. 1992. Health instruction responsibilities and competencies for elementary (K–6) classroom teachers. *Journal of School Health* 62, no. 2:76–77.

Joint Committee on Health Education Terminology. 1990. *Report of the 1990 Joint Committee on Health Education Terminology*. Reston, Va.: Association for the Advancement of Health Education.

Kreutter, K. J., H. Gewirtz, J. E. Davenny, and C. Love. 1991. Drug and alcohol prevention project for sixth graders: First-year findings. *Adolescence* 262:287–93.

Krueger, R. A. 1994. *Focus groups: A practical guide for applied research*. 2nd ed. Thousand Oaks, Calif.: Sage.

Lisnov, L., C. G. Harding, L. A. Safer, and J. Kavanagh. 1998. Adolescents' perceptions of substance abuse prevention strategies. *Adolescence* 33:301–11.

Pigg Jr., R. M. 1989. The contribution of school health programs to the broader goals of public health: The American experience. *Journal of School Health* 59, no. 1:25–30.

Shujaa, M. J. 1995. Cultural self meets cultural others in the African American experience: Teachers' responses to curriculum content reform. *Theory into Practice* 34:194–201.

Taylor, G. R. 1998. *Curriculum strategies for teaching social skills to the disabled: Dealing with inappropriate behavior*. Springfield, Ill.: Charles C. Thomas.

———. 1999. *Curriculum models and strategies for educating individuals with disabilities in inclusive classrooms*. Springfield, Ill.: Charles C. Thomas.

———. 2002. *Assessing children with disabilities*. New York: Edwin Mellen Press.

8

DRUG ABUSE AMONG HIGH-RISK MINORITY POPULATIONS

It is not within the scope of this chapter to trace the history of drug abuse among high-risk minority individuals or to imply that all minorities contain high-risk individuals; rather, this chapter is designed to show how high-risk factors are responsible for many minorities being classified as high risk. For purposes of this chapter, high-risk minority populations are defined as individuals who live in impoverished environments, are exposed to a high incidence of crime and drug use, have disabilities in several areas of functioning, have failed several grades, have a high incidence of health problems including diseases and malnutrition, or whose primary language may not be English. In addition, they may have a significant number of social and psychosocial problems, including teenage pregnancy, fatherless homes, and a high incidence of physical abuse. They are classified for the purpose of this chapter as African Americans, Hispanics, Native Americans, Pacific Islanders, and individuals with disabilities.

This chapter summarizes the prevalence of drug abuse as related to major minority groups in America. Data reported through this chapter supports the theory that there are significant similarities between and among the various groups, attributed to the causes and factors associated with drug abuse. Because populations of minority groups are

projected to significantly increase in the next decade, it may be concluded that drug abuse will also increase. It therefore becomes incumbent upon educational institutions to understand racial/ethnic patterns
of drug abuse and to design realistic drug prevention programs as reported in chapters 3, 6, and 8.

MINORITY GROUPS IN THE UNITED STATES

African American Males

National statistics indicate that addiction to drugs is on the increase
for African American males. Nearly one in three (32.2 percent) of them
in the age group twenty to twenty-nine (827,440) are under criminal justice supervision, in prison or jail, or on probation or parole. African
American males constitute 13 percent of all drug users who elect to use
drugs at least once per month. They represent 35 percent of all arrests
for drug possession, 55 percent of convictions, and 74 percent of prison
sentences (Mauer and Huling 1995; Greenwood 1992; Johnstone, O'-
Malley, and Bachman 1998; U.S. General Accounting Office 1993; U.S.
Department of Justice 1993).

The exact number of people using drugs is not known because many
of them are not apprehended or convicted. The increase in drug usage
and abuse among African American males, in particular, can be attributed to many factors; many are deeply rooted in the culture and various
types of personality conflicts that many African American males experience in our society (Grob and DeRios 1992; Newcomb and Bentler
1988; Shedler and Block 1990; Taylor 1972). Whatever the reasons for
this increase in drug usage among African Americans, society faces a
mammoth task in reversing this trend.

Part of the solution to reduce these dreadful statistics is to provide job
training and opportunities for African American males (especially in the
inner city), more antidrug programs, direct involvement of youths in
planning and structuring programs, and diversion programs that get
small-time users treatment, not jail. A significant number of research
studies have found a high correlation between the socioeconomic status
of young African American males and drug crimes (Botvin, Schinke, and

Orlandi 1995; Gordon, Gordon, and Nembhard 1995; Pandey and Coulton 1994; Short 1997; Manwar 1997).

Drug-related AIDS cases have significantly increased over the last several decades. AIDS and HIV-related infections associated with drug usage are significantly higher within this population when compared to other groups because of the sharing of hypodermic syringes (Substance Abuse and Mental Health Services Administration 1998).

Hispanics

Hispanic subgroups vary markedly in the prevalence of substance abuse, alcohol dependence, and need for illicit drug abuse treatment. Relative to the total U.S. population, Mexicans and Puerto Ricans have high usage rates of illicit drugs (including marijuana, cocaine, and other illicit drugs), heavy alcohol use, alcohol dependence, and the need for illicit drug abuse treatment. In contrast, Caribbean citizens, Central Americans, and Cubans have a low prevalence, and South Americans and other Hispanics have prevalence rates that are close to those of the total U.S. population. For example, the percentage of the population aged twelve and older using any illicit drugs in the past year equals about 13 percent among Mexicans and Puerto Ricans, 7.6 percent among Caribbean citizens, 5.7 percent among Central Americans, 8.2 percent among Cubans, and 11 percent among South Americans and other Hispanics, compared with about 12 percent in the total U.S. population (U. S. Department of Health and Human Services 2002; Rothe 2001; De la Rosa 1998; Vega and Gill 1998). With respect to past-year cigarette use, Puerto Ricans have a relatively high prevalence, Caribbean and Central American citizens have a relatively low prevalence, and Cubans, Mexicans, South Americans, and other Hispanics have an intermediate prevalence relative to the U.S. population (U.S. Department of Health and Human Services 2002; Rothe 2001; De la Rosa 1998; Vega and Gill 1998).

The reasons that Hispanics to use drugs are varied and complex, and different from Caucasians. Cultural barriers and poverty impede them from seeking appropriate drug treatment programs (Waters, Fazio, and Hernandez 2002; Strait 1999; Alaniz, Treno, and Salt 1999; Velez-Blasini 1997). Shedler and Deren (2002) voiced that the existence of ethnically and culturally diverse Hispanic communities indicate that qualitative research on HIV-related attitudes and behaviors within subgroups is needed to develop successful interventions (Delgado 1999). African Americans and Hispanics have the highest rates of AIDS-related diseases in the country. A knowledge of cultural norms can serve as a foundation for drug treatment programs and services. In addition, many Hispanics do not understand our complex legal system, due chiefly to language and culture differences. For specific information on drug abuse among Hispanic Americans, refer to Substance Abuse and Mental Health Services Administration (1998), "Prevalence of Substance Use among Racial and Ethnic Subgroups in the United States, 1991–1993."

Native Americans

Native Americans are persons having origins in and maintaining cultural identification with any of the original people of North America, including American Indian tribes and Alaskan natives. This report supports previous research in suggesting that, relative to the total U.S. population, Native Americans have a very high prevalence of past-year substance use (including cigarettes, alcohol, and illicit drugs), alcohol dependence, and the need for illicit drug abuse treatment. For example, about 53 percent of Native Americans aged twelve and older used cigarettes in the past year versus about 31 percent in the total U.S. population aged twelve and older. About 20 percent of Native Americans used an illicit drug in the past year (versus 12 percent of U.S. population), and about 7.8 percent were in need of illicit drug-abuse treatment (versus 2.7 percent) (U.S. Department of Health and Human Services 2002; Substance Abuse and Mental Health Services 1998).

American Indians and Alaska natives made up less than 1 percent of the U.S. population in 1999, yet they accounted for 2.4 percent of all admissions to drug treatment facilities. Alcohol was the primary substance of abuse for American Indians and Alaska natives. The alcoholism death rate according to Indian Health Services (1992, 1996, 1997) is higher for this group than the general population. The overall rates of substance use and abuse, according to several researchers, deviates from tribe to tribe (Stubben 1997; May 1982; Oetting and Beauvis 199; Dick, Manson, and Beals 1993). Alcohol accounted for 62 percent of all cases. Marijuana was the most common illicit drug among this population. A substantial number of Native Americans have severe alcohol problems. As with Hispanics, cultural barriers and poverty deter this population from seeking appropriate drug treatment programs as well as the development of appropriate drug programs (Substance Abuse and Mental Health Services Administration 1998).

Asian/Pacific Islanders

Asian and Pacific Islanders are individuals who trace their ancestries to Asia or the Pacific Islands. Individuals of Chinese, Japanese, or Filipino ancestry or origin accounted for about 60 percent of the Asian/Pacific Islander population. This report supports previous research in showing that Asian/Pacific Islanders' prevalence of substance use, alcohol dependence, and the need for illicit substance abuse treatment, while clearly high enough to warrant attention, is low relative to those of the total U.S. population. For example, the percentages of Asian/Pacific Islanders aged twelve and older who used cigarettes, alcohol, and any illicit drugs in the past year are about 22 percent, 53 percent, and 6.5 percent respectively, compared with about 31 percent, 66 percent, and 12 percent in the total U.S. population aged twelve and older. As in the total U.S. population, males have a higher prevalence than females for every substance, but the gender gap is larger among Asian/Pacific Islanders than in the total U.S. population. For example, the percentages of Asian/Pacific Islander males and females using cigarettes in the past year equal about 30 percent and 14 percent, respectively, as compared with 34 percent and 28 percent among males and females in the total U.S. population.

Given the extensive ethnic diversity of the Asian/Pacific Islander category used here, this data should be interpreted with caution; averages for the overall group mask significant variations in the prevalence of substance use among subgroups (Department of Health and Human Services 2002; Substance Abuse and Mental Health Services 1998). Recent findings have shown alarming incidents of substance abuse among different Asian ethnic groups. The heterogeneity of the group and cultural barriers have impeded research to gain exact knowledge concerning substance abuse. Treatment and interventions must consider cultural factors and family influences. This is deemed important because of the wide social, cultural, and diverse differences and makeup of various ethnic groups among this population, including Chinese, Koreans, Japanese, Filipinos, Pacific Islanders, Vietnamese, Thai, Cambodians, Laotians, and Indonesians (Jo 1993; Uehara, Takeuchi, and Smukler 1994; Ho 1994; Substance Abuse and Mental Health Services 1998).

Children with Disabilities

Children with disabilities cover a wide range of impairments in all major areas human functioning. Several classification systems list thirteen areas of disabilities:

- Autism
- Deaf-blindness
- Deafness
- Emotional disturbance
- Hearing impairment
- Mental retardation
- Multiple disabilities
- Orthopedic impairment
- Other health impairment
- Specific learning disabilities
- Speech or language
- Traumatic brain injury
- Visual impairment, including blindness

For a detailed description of these exceptionalities, refer to Ysseldyke, Algozzine, and Thurlow (1992) and Taylor (2001).

Children with disabilities may be found in all minority and high-risk groups, as well as the overall population. Drug treatments applicable to the minority groups discussed earlier may be modified and adapted to meet the unique needs of each disabled group. Reasons for the high rate of substance abuse among this group may be attributed to (1) poor self-image, (2) stress factors, (3) negative attitudes, (4) myths, (5) poorly trained professionals who are not well trained concerning the needs and characteristics of the group and who cannot provide appropriate treatment services, (6) lack of appropriate facilities, and (7) poorly constructed research designs (McGillicuddy and Blane 1999; Campbell, Essex, and Held 1994; Helwing and Holicky 1994; Ogborne and Smart 1995; Hubbard, Everett, and Khan 1996).

Recent statistics reveal that the greatest number of disabled students who are subjected to substance abuse have antisocial disorders. Disabled individuals who use chemical substances often display extreme difficulty in day-to-day functions at home and school. They frequently have poor interpersonal relationships, are easily frustrated, anxiety prone, hyperactive, impulsive, have low tolerance levels, poor judgment, mood disturbance, and frequently demonstrate violent behaviors. Drug education is just as necessary for children with disabilities as their "normal" peers. They frequently need additional assistance in resisting the urgings to use drugs from peer groups and to be taught how to distinguish the differences between appropriate use of drugs (medications) and inappropriate drug use (Guthmann 1996; McCrone 1994).

AIDS AND DRUG USE

The number of individuals affected with AIDS has increased rapidly throughout the country in the last several years. Infection appears to be highest among high-risk groups (Sullivan 1996; Fisher and Fisher 1992). Human immunodeficiency virus (HIV) systematically destroys the immune system of the body, thus resulting in a wide variety of infections. The causes, effects, and treatment of AIDS have been adequately reported in other sources and will not be elaborated upon in this chapter. The reader is referred to Stimmel (1993).

Testing for HIV in intravenous drug users (IVDUs) is of the highest importance in helping to prevent the transmission of AIDS. Needle sharing among IVDUs has contributed significantly to the number of individuals affected. Attempts on the local, state, and federal levels had been made to reduce the transmission of HIV through intravenous drug use. Some of the practices have included education programs, distribution of disinfected and sterile needles, and treatment programs (Boatler, Knight, and Simpson 1994; Holtgrave and Qualls 1995; Mann 1991).

Educational personnel must be educated about HIV disease and the potential long-term needs of the infected student. All schools should have programs for educating youths in standard precautions and in recognizing and managing medical emergencies. Some children with HIV infections will need medical treatment while in school (American Academy of Pediatrics 1990, 1993, 1998). School experiences are deemed necessary and important for children with HIV infections in order to develop and promote their social growth. They should be included in as many activities as their physical conditions will permit. For those children too ill to attend school, home instruction should be provided, as mandated under federal laws (American Academy of Pediatrics 1990). Refer to Taylor (2001) for detailed information on federal laws.

HIV infection is linked to sharing infected needles. This infection may be the result of an intravenous drug user passing on the needle to be reused, thereby transmitting the needle with infected blood to another user. These conditions increase significantly the transmission of HIV infection. Once infected, an intravenous drug user can pass infections to others through needle sharing or sexual contact. Prevention programs are needed to assist in lowering the large percentage of youths affected by HIV (Rotheram-Borus and Miller 1998; Friedman, Curtis, Jose, and Neaigus 1997; U.S. Department of Health and Human Services 1999; Korber and Myers 1992; Mann 1991; McKoy and Inciardi 1995; Wight 1992; Sullivan 1996; Holtgrave and Qualls 1995; Fisher and Fisher 1992; Kelly, St. Lawrence, Hood, and Brasfield 1989; Boatler, Knight, and Simpson 1994; American Academy of Pediatrics 1997, 1999).

SOCIOECONOMIC FACTORS AND DRUG CRIMES

To find some of the causes of the incarceration of high numbers of minorities and high-risk youths, a number of studies found correlations between socioeconomic status, ethnicity/race, and drug-related crime. Gordon, Gordon, and Nembhard (1995) concluded an extensive review of the literature from 1955 through 1994 on African American males and their involvement in a variety of social problems. Studies focusing on demographic factors have repeatedly shown that urban, young, unemployed youths and minorities of lower socioeconomic status tend to cope with social conditions by drinking alcohol and using drugs. Also, many of these males become involved in crimes that are drug related. The socioeconomic conditions among minority groups are significantly contributing to them becoming at risk for drug abuse, which may lead to health risks, criminal behavior, and reduced chances for improving their socioeconomic conditions.

In another study conducted in Cleveland, Pandey and Coulton (1994) found that as neighborhoods declined, they became more populated by lower socioeconomic groups of minorities. Soon drug-related crimes began to increase, as did the number of nondrug-related crimes. It was also found that the incidence and the number of nondrug-related crimes were higher among groups away from the mainstream and dominant culture of White America.

Bailey, Hser, Hsieh, and Anglin (1994) studied minorities involved in drug crimes by following 354 narcotics addicts remanded to the California Civil Addict Program from 1962 through 1964 for a period of twenty-four years. Self-reported data collected at initial treatment admission and in two follow-up interviews (1974–1975 and 1985–1986) included information on family history, patterns of drug use, criminal involvement, socioeconomic status, and other behavioral and sociodemographic differences. This study supported the basic premise that the social environment plays a dominant role in promoting criminal behavior. Data showed that criminal involvement is directly related to drug usage among prison inmates.

SOCIODEMOGRAPHIC DIFFERENCES IN SUBSTANCE USE

Sociodemographic differences among racial/ethnic subgroups explain, at least in part, the subgroups' different prevalence of substance use, alcohol dependence, and need for illicit drug abuse treatment (Strait 1999). For example, relative to the total U.S. population, individuals in households with low family income have a high prevalence of past-year use of any illicit drugs, and the percentage of population with low family income is higher among Mexicans, non-Hispanic Blacks, and Puerto Ricans than in the total U.S. population. Thus, family income differences partially account for the relatively high prevalence of illicit drug use among Mexicans, Puerto Ricans, and non-Hispanic Blacks. Yet, none of the sociodemographic variables that are introduced in analyses, including region, population density, language of interview, family income, health insurance coverage, receipt of welfare, educational attainment, school dropout status, marital status, employment status, and number of children, fully accounts for racial/ethnic difference in substance use. Regardless of racial/ethnic subgroup, a relatively high prevalence of illicit drug use is found among individuals who reside in the West, reside in metropolitan areas with populations greater than 1 million, use English rather than Spanish, lack health insurance coverage, are unemployed, have nine to eleven years of schooling, or have never been married. Moreover, regardless of racial/ethnic subgroup, adolescents who dropped out of school or who reside in households with only one biological parent have a relatively high prevalence of past-year use of cigarettes, alcohol, and illicit drugs (U.S. Department of Health and Human Services 2002; Substance Abuse and Mental Health Services Administration 1998; Kling and Thayer 1993).

Dropout rates are magnified for homeless minority youths, throwaway teens, those living on the streets, inner-city gang members, and youths from fatherless and non-English speaking family backgrounds (Newcomb and Bentler 1988; U.S. Department of Education 1994; U.S. Department of Health and Human Services, 1999; Sasao 1992). Dropout rates in general are higher than the national average, with African Americans and Hispanics constituting the highest rates. Similarly, dropout rates for Native Americans are high, while those for Asian American youths are very low (U.S. Department of Education 1994).

COMMONALITIES AND DIFFERENCES AMONG MINORITY POPULATIONS

A Gestalt position that has been embraced by many citizens is that America is an umbrella social system, where cultures and traditions blend into one all-inclusive community, reflective of common goals, opportunities, and experiences. Although the various racial/ethnic groups in the United

States may share a common culture, with many similarities in areas such as values, spirituality, family functioning, and language, there are important sociodemographic differences (e.g., country of origin, level of education, and acculturation level) that may explain why a consensus model of ethnic and cultural melding has remained theoretical and underdeveloped. Researchers must acknowledge and then accept that groups retain their own values, belief, and behavior systems and that the cultural diversity within these groups has been generally overlooked.

When classifying ethnic minority status, general population categories have traditionally been defined as (1) Blacks or African Americans, (2) Hispanics, (3) Native Americans or American Indians, (4) Asians or Pacific Islanders, and (5) individuals with disabilities. This simplified division has produced epidemiological and etiological data delineating major sociodemographic differences across these communities and has enabled researchers to study each population as if it were an unvarying, cohesive whole—a distinct culture. However, nested within each group are a variety of cultural variations, traditions, and styles that are as distinct and different as constructs measured across populations (National Institutes of Health Guide 1996).

As such, there is no Black or African American community; there are individuals who are descendants of American slaves, foreign-born Blacks, and individuals who are racially mixed. The Hispanic group includes Puerto Ricans, Mexican Americans, Cubans, Central and Latin Americans, and individuals from Spain. Likewise, the Native American group is not one homogenous community; there are a variety of Southwestern, Northern Plains, Eastern Woodlands, and Pacific Northwestern groups. The most complex, and the least studied, are the Asian and Pacific Islander populations, which consist of individuals from twenty-six countries/island groups and who had the fastest growth rate (82 percent) of any group in the 1980s. The 2000 census data are similar to the 1980s data. The 2000 census shows that America is becoming more racially and ethnically diverse. Asian and Pacific Northwestern groups increased from 8.2 percent in 1980 to 18.9 percent in 2000 (U.S. Department of Commerce News 2003). Individuals with disabilities appear in all of these groups.

Prevention intervention research needs to address diverse culturally relevant contexts and drug abuse etiologies for at-risk groups. For example, population studies indicate that American Indians, particularly those on reservations, have the highest rates of drug abuse compared with any other minority group. Is this statistic a commonality across all American Indians or is it specific to the Southwestern tribes? What are the implications for the design and testing of prevention interventions? Research focused on the role of acculturation suggests that Puerto Rican youths who identified less with Puerto Rican cultural values were more likely to abuse drugs than those who were more identified. Is acculturation strain equivocal across all Hispanic groups (e.g., Mexican Americans) and does it impact on initiation of drug abuse to the same extent? What prevention interventions could be developed and tested to address social adaptation issues? Data show that African Americans are more likely to use drugs intravenously. Is this pattern consistent for foreign-born as well as American-born Blacks? What are the key factors promoting IV drug abuse and are these factors amenable to change through prevention interventions? Attitudes regarding health and addiction within the Asian and Pacific Islander groups and Native American Indians also vary greatly. For example, Samoans do not view drug abuse as an addiction, but as an episodic mistake in the judgment of the user. This interpretation of the nature of addiction is incompatible with the beliefs of other Asian cultures that consider drug abuse as an imbalance in spiritual matters. To what extent can prevention interventions address drug-related belief structures that are indigenous to a cultural and disability areas? Notwithstanding some shared, basic underlying cultural similarities across minority groups, there are very real within-group differences (e.g., rituals, values, attitudes, etc.) that make it crucial to fine-tune existing prevention intervention research efforts (National Institute of Health Guide 1996; Strait 1999; Walters 2002; Hubbard, Everett, and Khan 1996; Kling and Thayer 1993; Oetting and Beauvis 1989; Jo 1993; Shedler and Deren 2002; May 1982).

GENDER EFFECTS

A scarcity of prevention intervention research addresses the unique set of physical, biological, social, and psychological problems that are specific to women in all minority groups. (The term *woman* is used to refer to females of all ages. Elsewhere, where appropriate, the terms *girl* and *adolescent females* are used.) Although females comprise 51 percent of the population, they have been neglected in this field of research, and therefore, unserved as a group distinct from males. Gender differences in the epidemiology of drug abuse are quite apparent, with the number of male drug abusers and addicts exceeding that of females. The consequences of drug abuse by women, however, are more severe and data indicates that, after initial use, women may proceed more rapidly to drug abuse than men. The causes, correlates, and consequences of drug abuse and addiction appear also to differ with respect to men and women. For women, for example, a fairly high correlation appears to exist between eating disorders and substance abuse. Preliminary research data from the National Institute on Drug Abuse (NIDA) indicates that the more severely a woman diets and engages in binge eating, the more likely she is to experience negative consequences from drinking alcohol, and the more likely she is to meet the criteria for substance abuse or dependence (National Institutes of Health 1996; Helwing and Holicky 1994; Campbell, Essex, and Held 1994; McGillicuddy and Blane 1999; Dick, Manson, and Beal 1993).

Women's initiation into drug use also differs from that of men. Preliminary results from a study on gender differences in cocaine initiation and abuse indicate that approximately 90 percent of women reported that men played some role in their involvement with crack cocaine. By contrast, only 17 percent of men reported that women were involved in their initiating or maintaining cocaine use in order to develop more intimate relationships, while men were more likely to use the drug with male friends and in relation to the drug trade. With regard to antecedent conditions, although conduct disorders and other observable behaviors signal risk for males, the etiology of female drug abuse appears to lie in predisposing psychiatric disorders prior to abusing drugs. Preliminary data from studies of antecedents of crack cocaine abuse among African American women found preexisting psychiatric problems to be a major cofactor. Specifically, there was a strong correlation between the age of first drug use and the first depressive episode. Additionally, these women had conflicting relationships with, and less attachment to, their mothers (National Institutes of Health Guide 1996).

Women who have been victims of crime, likewise, appear to have increased vulnerability to substance abuse. Research conducted among a population of women in residential or outpatient drug treatment programs found that 80 percent had been crime victims. Additionally, female crime victims were more likely to have major drug and alcohol problems than nonvictims. Female crime victims who suffered from post traumatic stress disorder (PTSD) were almost ten times more likely to have major alcohol problems and seventeen times more likely to have major drug abuse problems than nonvictims. Numerous studies have shown PTSD to be a strong predictor of substance abuse.

Many questions remain to be addressed regarding prevention intervention activities for females and disabled individuals. For example, to what extent does initiation of drug use and progression from use to abuse and dependence differ for females when compared to males? How does drug use differ among and across different disability groups? Are specific techniques and strategies needed for each disability group? To what degree this occurs will provide important information that needs to be incorporated in targeted drug prevention intervention efforts. Different types of victimization (e.g., sexual abuse, physical abuse, being the child of a drug-abusing mother or father, etc.) create different patterns of subsequent drug abuse. How should prevention interventions differ as a function of this? Does the descent from various ethnic cultures and disability groups promote specific native gender roles and to what extent are these congruent, complementary, or in conflict with society at large? The scientific answers to these and many other questions are necessary to advance prevention intervention activities (National Institutes of Health Guide 1996).

SUMMARY

Research initiatives seek to identify risk and protective factors in order to design and test comprehensive, theory-based preventive interventions that are sensitive to cultural norms and responsive to community needs (Sisson 1981). Prevention intervention research should focus upon the strengths of cultural systems as experienced and promulgated by the family and community. For example, research is needed to know how positive family sanctions and strong religious values may protect culturally diverse and disabled youths from drugs or abuse during their early school years. (Refer to chapter 9 for a proposed evaluation model.) Prevention intervention research is needed to know how family values and community networks of friends, volunteers, and relatives interact. Research is needed to design and test promising drug prevention programs that build upon the cultural, social, family, and religious values that appear to protect or inoculate many culturally diverse and disabled youths from drug abuse and HIV/AIDS. Prevention intervention strategies for these groups should entail a comprehensive approach to their needs at the universal, selective, and indicated levels (National Institute of Health Guide 1996; Rothe 2001; Botvin, Schinke, and Orlandi 1995; Substance Abuse and Mental Health 1998; Grob and DeRios 1992; Stubben 1997).

REFERENCES

Alaniz, M. L., A. J. Treno, and R. F. Saltz. 1999. Gender, acculturation, and alcohol consumption among Mexican Americans. *Substance Use Misuse* 34, no. 10:1407–26.

American Academic of Pediatrics. 1990. Committee on School Health: Guidelines for urging care in school. *Pediatrics* 86: 999–1000.

———. 1993. Committee on School Health: Guidelines for the administration of medication in school. *Pediatrics* 92: 499–500.

———. 1997. HIV infection. In *1997 Red Book Report of the Committee on Infectious Diseases*, edited by G. Peter. 24th ed. Elk Grove Village, Ill.: American Academy of Pediatrics.

———. 1998. Human immunodeficiency virus/acquired immunodeficiency syndrome education in schools. *Pediatrics* 101 933–35.

———. 1999. Issues related to human immunodeficiency virus transmission in schools, child care, medical settings, the home, and community. *Pediatrics* 104:318–24.

Bailey, R. C., Y. Hser, S. Hsieh, and M. D. Anglin. 1994. Influences affecting maintenance and cessation of narcotics addiction. Special issues: Drugs and crime revised. *Journal of Drug Issues* 24, no. 12:249–72.

Boatler, J. F., K. Knight, and D. D. Simpson. 1994. Assessment of an AIDS intervention program during drug abuse treatment. *Journal of Substance Abuse Treatment* 11, no. 4 (August): 367–72.

Botvin, G. J., S. Schinke, and M. A. Orlandi, eds. 1995. *Drug abuse prevention with multiethnic youth*. Thousand Oaks, Calif.: Sage.

Campbell, J. A., E. L. Essex, and G. Held. 1994. Issues in chemical dependency treatment and aftercare for people with learning differences: Part of a special issue on chemical dependency. *Health and Social Work* 19:63–70.

De la Rosa, M. R. 1998. Prevalence and consequences of alcohol, cigarette, and drug use among Hispanics. *Alcoholism Treatment Quarterly* 16, no. 1–2:21–54.

Delgado, M. 1999. Involvement of the Hispanic community in ATOD research. *Drugs and Society* 14, no. 1–2:93–105.

Dick, R. W., S. M. Manson, and J. Beals. 1993. Alcohol use among male and female Native American adolescents: Patterns and correlates of student drinking in a boarding school. *Journal of Studies on Alcohol* 54:172–77.

Fisher, J. D., and W. A. Fisher. 1992. Changing AIDS risk behavior. *Psychological Bulletin* 111, no. 3 (May): 455–74.

Friedman, S. R., R. Curtis, B. Jose, and A. Neaigus. 1997. Parentally and sexually transmitted diseases in high risk neighborhoods. *Sexually Transmitted Disease* 24:322–26.

Gordon, E. T., E. W. Gordon, and J. G. Nembhard. 1995. Social science literature concerning African American men. *Journal of Negro Education* 63, no. 4:508–31. Special Issue.

Greenwood, P. 1992. Substance abuse among high-risk youth and potential intervention. *Crime and Delinquency* 38, no. 4:444–58.

Grob, C., and M. D. DeRios. 1992. Adolescent drug use in cross-cultural perspective. *Journal of Drug Issues* 22, no. 1:126–39.

Guthmann, D. 1996. An analysis of variables that impact treatment outcomes of chemically dependent deaf and hard of hearing individuals. University of Minnesota, Minneapolis: *Dissertation Abstracts International* 56, no. 7A:2638.

Helwing, A. A., and R. Holicky. 1994. Substance abuse in persons with disabilities: Treatment consideration. *Journal of Counseling and Development* 72, no. 3 (January–February): 227–33.

Ho, M. K. 1994. *Managing multiculturalism in substance abuse service.* Thousand Oaks, Calif.: Sage.

Holtgrave, D. R., and N. L. Qualls. 1995. Threshold analysis and program for prevention of HIV infection. *Medical Decision Making* 14, no. 4 (October–December): 311–17.

Indian Health Service. 1992. *Trends in Indian health—1991.* Rockville, Md.: Indian Health Service.

———. 1996. *Trends in Indian health—1995.* Rockville, Md.: Indian Health Service.

Jo, D.Y., Aoki. 1993. Substance abuse treatment: Cultural behaviors in the Asian American community. *Journal of Psychoactive Drugs* 25, no. 1:61–71.

Johnson, L. D., P. M. O'Malley, and J. G. Bachman. 1998. *National survey results on drug use for monitoring the future study.* Rockville, Md. U.S. Department of Health and Human Services.

Hubbard, J. R., A. S. Everett, and M. Khan. 1996. Alcohol and drug abuse in patients with physical disabilities. *American Journal of Drug and Alcohol Abuse* 22 (May): 215–31.

Kelly, J. A., J. S. St. Lawrence, H. V. Hood, and T. L. Brasfield. 1989. Behavioral intervention to reduce AIDS risk activities. Journal *of Counseling Psychology* 57, no. 1 (February): 60–67.

Kling, J., and J. Thayer. 1993. Examining contextual models for understanding drug use behavior among American Indian youth. In *Prevention of mental disorders, alcohol, and other drug use in children and adolescents*, edited by D. Shafer, I. Phillips, and N. Enzer, 129–43. Washington, D.C.: U.S. Department of Health and Human Services. DHHS Publication no. (ADM) 92-1646.

Korber, B., and G. Myers. 1992. Signature pattern analysis: A method for assessing viral sequence relatedness. *AIDS Prevention in Human Retroviruses* 8:1549–60.

Mann, J. M. 1991. Global AIDS: Critical issues for prevention in the 1990s. *International Journal of Health Services* 21, no. 3:553–59.

Manwar, A. 1997. Social construction of self among the New York City crack dealers. A paper presented at a meeting of the Society for the Study of Social Problems. New York: National Development and Research Institutes.

Mauer, M., and T. Huling. 1995. Young black Americans and the criminal justice system: Five years later. *The sentencing project*. Washington, D.C.: U.S. Department of Justice.

May, P. A. 1982. Substance abuse and American Indians: Prevalence and susceptibility. *The International Journal of the Addictions* 17, no. 7:1185–209.

McCrone, W. 1994. A two-year report card on Title I of the American Disabilities Act: Implications for rehabilitation counseling with deaf people. *Journal of American Deafness and Rehabilitation Association* 28, no. 2:1–20.

McKoy, C. B., and J. A. Inciardi. 1995. *Sex, drugs, and the spread of AIDS*. Los Angeles, Calif.: Roxburg.

McGillicuddy, N. B., and H. T. Blane. 1999. Substance use in individuals with mental retardation. *Addictive Behaviors* 24, no. 6 (November–December): 869–78.

National Institutes of Health Guide. 1996. *Drug abuse prevention for women and minorities* 25, no. 2.

Newcomb, M., and P. Bentler. 1988. *Consequences of adolescent drug use: Impact on the lives of young adults*. Newbury Park, Calif.: Sage.

Oetting, E., and F. Beauvis. 1989. Epidemiology and correlates of alcohol use among Indian adolescents living on reservations. In *Alcohol use among U.S. ethnic minorities*, 239–67. Rockville, Md.: U.S. Department of Health and Human Services.

Ogborne, A. C., and R. G. Smart. 1995. People with physical disabilities admitted to a residential addiction treatment program. *American Journal of Drug and Alcohol Abuse* 21, no. 1 (February): 137–45.

Pandey, S., and C. Coulton. 1994. Unraveling neighborhood change using two-wave panel analysis: A case study of Cleveland in the 1980s. *Social Work Research* 18, no. 2:83–96.

Rothe, E. M. 2001. *Ethnocultural factors in substance abuse treatment.* New York: Guilford Press.

Rotheram-Borus, M. J., and S. Miller. 1998. Secondary prevention for youth living with HIV. *Behavioral Medicine* 10, no. 11:17–34.

Sasao, T. 1992. *Substance abuse and gang violence*, edited by R. C. Cervantes. Newbury Park, Calif.: Sage.

Shedler, J., and J. Block. 1990. Adolescent drug use and psychological health: A longitudinal inquiry. *American Psychologist* 45, no. 6:612–30.

Shedler, M. G., and S. Deren. 2002. Cultural factors in influencing HIV risk behavior among Dominicans in New York City. *Journal of Ethnicity in Substance Abuse* 1, no. 1:71–95.

Short, J. F. 1997. *Poverty, ethnicity, and violent crime.* Boulder, Colo.: Westview Press.

Sisson, R. W. 1981. *The effect of three relaxation procedures on tension reduction and subsequent drinking of inpatient alcoholics.* Unpublished Ph.d diss., Southern Illinois University at Carbondale. Carbondale, Ill.: University Microfilms No. 8122668.

Strait, S. C. 1999. Drug use among Hispanic youth: Examining common unique contributing factors. *Hispanic Journal of Behavioral Sciences* 21, no. 1 (February): 89–103.

Stubben, J. 1997. Culturally competent substance abuse prevention research among rural Native American communities. In *Rural substance abuse: State knowledge and issues*, edited by E. Robertson, Z. Sloboda, G. Boyd, L. Beatty, and N. Kozel, 459–83. Washington, D.C.: U.S. Department of Health and Human Services. NIH Publication no. 97-4177.

Substance Abuse and Mental Health Services Administration. 1998. *Prevalence of substance abuse use among racial and ethnic subgroups in the United States, 1991–1993.* Washington, D.C.: U.S. Government Printing Office.

Sullivan, T. R. 1996. The challenge of HIV prevention among high-risk adolescents. *Health Social Work* 21, no. 1:58–65.

Taylor, G. R. 1972. Toward a model K–12 program in drug education. *Thrust for Education Leadership* 1, no. 42:28–32.

———. 2001. *Educational services and strategies for educating individuals with exceptionalities.* Springfield, Ill.: Charles C. Thomas.

Uehara, E. S., D. T. Takeuchi, and M. Smukler. 1994. *American Journal of Community Psychology* 22, no. 1 (February): 83–99.

U.S. Department of Commerce News. 2003. At www.census.gov/press_release/www/2003/cb03143.html (accessed October 1, 2003).

U.S. Department of Education. 1994. *Reaching the goals: Goal 2—High school completion. Defining dropouts: A statistical portrait.* Washington, D.C.: U.S. Government Printing Office.

U.S. Department of Health and Human Services. 1999. *Young teens: Who they are and how to communicate with them about alcohol and other drugs.* Rockville, Md.: U.S. Department of Health and Human Services, Substance Abuse and Mental Health Administration, Center for Substance Abuse Prevention.

U.S. Department of Justice, Bureau of Justice Statistics. 1993. *Sentencing in the federal courts: Does race matter? The transition to sentencing guidelines, 1986–1990.* Washington, D.C.: U.S. Government Printing Office.

———. 1996. *National correction reporting program.* Washington, D.C.: U.S. Government Printing Office.

U.S. General Accounting Office. 1993. *Drug use among youth: No simple answers to guide prevention.* Washington, D.C.: U.S. General Accounting Office.

Vega, W. A., and A. G. Gil. 1998. *Drug use and ethnicity in early adolescence.* New York: Plenum Press.

Velez-Blasini, C. J. 1997. A cross-cultural comparison of alcohol expectations in Puerto Rico and the United States. *Psychological Addictive Behavior* 11:124–41.

Waters, J. A., S. L. Fazio, and L. Hernandez. 2002. The story of CURA, a Hispanic/Latino drug therapeutic community. *Journal of Ethnicity in Substance Abuse* 1, no. 1:113–34.

Wight, D. 1992. Impediments to safe heterosexual sex: A review of research with young pupils. *AIDS Care* 4, no. 11:11–23.

Ysseldyke, J., B. Algozzine, and M. Thurlow. 1992. *Critical issues in special education.* Boston, Mass.: Houghton Mifflin.

9

EVALUATING DRUG PROGRAMS

Evaluation is the process of determining relative worth. This is usually done by comparing an established standard with something of unknown value. In the case of evaluating drug usage, the investigator is attempting to assess the drug habits of individuals and the factors contributing to its use. Once this has been done, the adequacy of the hypothesis under study can be stated in terms of the responses of individuals. These responses may be categorized, with numerical values assigned and appropriate statistics selected to test the hypotheses. Analyses of the data will determine the effectiveness of the program in reducing drug usage.

Investigators and researchers must be competent in statistical and research methods. They should also use the objectives of the program as the safe evaluative criteria; make appropriate interpretation from the data presented—in essence, be objective in analyzing the data, make a judgment about individual responses regarding the usage (or the lack thereof) of drugs, and be able to give constructive feedback relevant to the analysis of the project.

Evaluation of a drug program is essential to prevention efforts. The ultimate goal is to prevent youths from using drugs. Consequently, the evaluation process for drug prevention programs is somewhat different from that for evaluating other programs. Specific instruments must be developed to ascertain attitudes toward drugs, such as questionnaires, surveys, teacher-made tests, checklists, and rating scales (Taylor 2002). Investigators should ensure that youths understand drug information and the harmful effects of drugs in order to determine whether perceptions concerning drugs have changed over time. Evaluation is crucial in preventing drug use for the following reasons:

1. It serves as a source of accounting for funds spent.
2. It can provide information on the types of instruments to use.
3. It provides information to organizations funding programs.
4. It can provide information on types of intervention relevant to how funds were expended.
5. It can provide information on appropriate statistics to use.
6. It yields information on strategies to employ in prevention programs.
7. It can provide a foundation for additional financial support by providing evidence of its effectiveness.
8. It indicates which strategies are successful on various populations.
9. It provides information for curriculum development.
10. It can provide a blueprint for school districts to replicate.

MAJOR TYPES OF EVALUATIONS

In addition to the reasons cited, process evaluation provides information to stakeholders regarding the effectiveness of the program; output evaluation indicates how many individuals were served; impact evaluation denotes whether the stated goals have been achieved; and outcomes evaluation measures the effects of long-term prevention in youths using drugs and the criminal activities associated with drugs. An effective evaluation should include the above four components in order to assess progress toward goals and objectives, and to refine strategies based upon results. It is incumbent upon the investigator to ensure that the evaluation model is connected to the objectives and expected outcomes of the program, and that sufficient time has been given between the pre- and post-assessment for determining the effectiveness of the program. Additionally, the evaluator must ensure that appropriate resources are available to ensure the success of the program (Ralph and

McMenamy 1996; Weiner, Prichard, et al. 1993; Kethmeni, Leamy, and Guyon 1991).

THE EVALUATION PROCESS

The evaluation process should include the following components: (1) a description of the way in which the curriculum and related activities are delivered, (2) a determination as to whether students have understood information about drugs and their consequences, and (3) an assessment of whether students' attitudes or drug behaviors have changed as a result of participating in the program.

Effective evaluation should involve the application of the scientific method in order to obtain realistic information relevant to drug use. The process should begin with observations and proceed through empirical testing, and answering research questions posed by the hypothesis. Both quantitative and qualitative methods may be used, with appropriate controls to determine whether the stated research questions or hypotheses have been answered. The research design should be clear so that other investigators can replicate the study (Taylor 2000).

Evaluation of a drug intervention process should be a continuous process based upon functional, realistic, and measurable objectives, as indicated in chapter 8. Effective evaluation necessitates that researchers understand drug prevention theory, concepts, strategies, and implementations. Educators can use a variety of instruments to assess the effectiveness of the program. The research design should match the program's objectives and, where the program is designed to make specific changes in students, these changes should be the basics for the evaluation. The success of these intervention programs cannot be fully realized until some initial assessment is made before students are exposed to the intervention. Evaluators need to be careful in analyzing and interpreting data, as well as drawing conclusions. (Refer to appendix F for evaluation resources.) It is almost impossible to determine the effectiveness of the program unless the aforementioned steps are completed. In order to determine the full impact of a drug program, students and community personnel attitudes and knowledge must be fully assessed. Well-developed evaluation guidelines are needed to effectively judge the worth of a drug curriculum.

DEVELOPMENT OF GUIDELINES

The following guidelines will assist evaluators in assessing and evaluating the effectiveness of drug programs:

1. Assess prior attitudes and knowledge toward the drug problem through tests, quizzes, surveys, debates, and class presentations.
2. Be sure your goals are reasonable and relevant.
3. List the objectives of the program in observable and measurable terms, based upon student, school, and community input.
4. List the methods of evaluation. Instruments such as objective tests, teacher-made tests, checklists, rating scales, attitudinal scales, and questionnaires may be instituted. These instruments should be administered on a pre- and post-test basis, be directly associated with the program's objectives, and be designed to determine the effectiveness of the drug program.
5. Determine what kinds of information you need to collect.
6. Determine what you will do with the information once you collect it and consider the analysis.
7. Call together the individuals responsible for collecting the information to be sure everyone knows what's supposed to happen, when, and why.
8. Conduct pretests. Also collect data that you want to use as bases for comparisons later.
9. Document responses of teachers and students concerning the program.
10. Document any events that may have had an impact on the evaluation.
11. Analyze the data. Always keep in mind the objectives of your program.
12. Interpret the data and include a description of the program, including its goals and objectives; a description of the audience

and setting; a description of the methods you used to conduct the evaluation; a description of the results, including both quantitative and qualitative data (Taylor 2000); a description of what these results say about the effectiveness of the program; and a description of how you plan to improve the program in the forthcoming year.

13. Disseminate the information.
14. Implement the needed changes in next year's program.

Several drug programs attempted to evaluate their effectiveness but did not adhere to the listed guidelines. Students and community individuals were assessed at the end of the program only. There were no indications that a precriterion test on any of these guidelines was followed to assess initial knowledge. Inadequate sampling, measurement, and data collection procedures were evident. The success of these programs in terms of assisting young people cannot be fully realized until some initial assessment is made before youths enter a drug education program. It is almost impossible to determine whether one program is more effective, acceptable, or efficient than another because of the lack of adequate evaluation procedures (Weiner, Prichard, et al. 1993; Aniskiewicz and Wysong 1990; Hansen and McNeal 1997; Zagummy and Thompson 1997; Falco 1994).

Implementing these steps will do much to reduce the controversy in evaluating drug abuse programs through increasing empirical results based upon weak research designs, including poor sampling techniques, the absence of a control group, improper intervention, and poor data collection procedures and measurement instrument and data analysis techniques. Most drug program evaluations do not follow an approved research paradigm. Seldom is a pre-test given before the intervention program; only a post-test is given after the intervention. It is virtually impossible to determine the effectiveness of a program using this incomplete model (Correll 1990; Silvia 1991; Taylor 2000; Wysong, Aniskiewicz, and Wright 1994; McMahon and Wuoreman 1992; McDonald, Towberman, and Hague 1990; Dukes, Stein, and Ullman 1996; Fife 1994; Wiegand 1991; Harmon 1993; Murray and Hannan 1990; Kethmeni, Leamy, and Guyon 1991; Bruvold and Randall 1998; Cook and Campbell 1979; Bangert-Drowns 1988; Weiner, Prichard, et al.

1993). Evaluation results from the Drug Abuse Resistance Education (D.A.R.E.) program, which is one of the largest drug programs in the country, showed little evidence for reducing substance abuse (Dejong 1987; Kochis 1993; Nyre 1984; Dukes, Stein, and Ullman 1996). Much of the failure can be attributed to poor research designs, lack of appropriate instruments, short timing periods in which to conduct the experiment, and a lack of youth and community involvement.

What is needed is a functional evaluation designed to correct some of the flaws in past evaluation designs and assessments. Stakeholders should collaborate in developing the model.

The proposed evaluation model will assist school districts and administrators in successfully evaluating intervention strategies.

Table 9.1. A Proposed Evaluation Model for Assessing Intervention Strategies

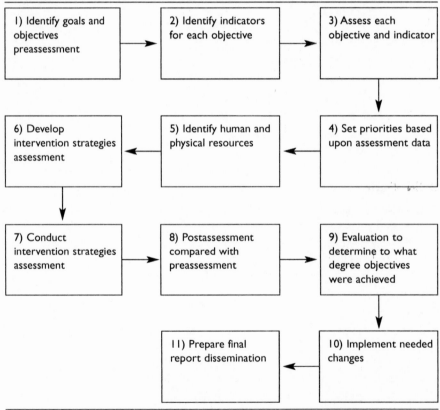

During the implementation of this model, some initial assessment should be made from which functional objectives can be developed.

- List indicators for each objective.
- Assess the value of objectives and indicators through surveying schools, teachers, and the community.
- From the assessed needs to carry out the strategies, conduct the intervention, and set time limits and standards.
- Compare preassessment data with postassessment data to determine the effectiveness of the strategies.
- Write the narrative report and disseminate results to stakeholders.

SUMMARY

Evaluation is the process of determining relative worth. Evaluation of drug programs is somewhat differs from evaluating other programs, in that the evaluator is attempting to assess the drug habits of individuals based upon the objectives of the program. Specific instruments must be developed to determine to what degree the stated objectives have been met. A variety of instruments and techniques can be developed, such as teacher-made tests, observations, checklists, surveys, questionnaires, and rating scales. The effectiveness of drug programs should show gains in students' drug knowledge, a reduction in drug usage, a change in perception of drug usage, and a positive change in drug-use behaviors.

Evaluation criteria and objectives should be developed and used to measure the effectiveness of the program, along with specific guidelines endorsed by all stakeholders. An evaluation model as outlined in this chapter is highly recommended in evaluating drug programs. Employing the strategies discussed in this chapter will do much to improving the evaluation results of drug education programs.

REFERENCES

Aniskiewicz, R. E., and E. E. Wysong. 1990. Evaluating D.A.R.E.: Drug education and the multiple meanings of success. *Policy Studies Reviews* 9, no. 4: 727–47.

Bangert-Drowns, R. L. 1988. The effects of school-based substance abuse education a meta-analysis. *Journal of Drug Education* 18: 243–65.

Bruvold, W. H., and T. G. Randall. 1988. A meta-analysis and theoretical review of school-based tobacco and alcohol intervention programs. *Psychology and Health* 2: 53–78.

Cook, T. D., and D. T. Campbell. 1979. *Quasi-experimentation: Design and analysis issues for field settings.* Chicago, Ill.: Rand McNally.

Correll, J. I. 1990. *Drug Abuse Resistance Education D.A.R.E.* Washington, D.C.: Department of Defense Dependents-M Evaluation Report.

Dejong, W. 1987. A short-term evaluation of Project D.A.R.E. Preliminary indicators of effectiveness. *Journal of Drug Education* 17, no. 4: 279–94.

Dukes, R. L., J. Stein, and J. Ullman. 1996. The long-term effects of D.A.R.E. *Evaluation Review* 20: 49–66.

———. 1996. Three-year follow-up of drug abuse resistance education. *Evaluation Review* 20: 49–66.

Falco, M. 1994. *The making of a drug-free America: Programs that work.* New York: Times Books.

Fife, B. L. 1994. *An assessment of the D.A.R.E. Program in Fort Wayne.* Fort Wayne, Ind.: Ball State University, Department of Political Science.

Hansen, W. B., and R. B. McNeal. 1997. How D.A.R.E. works: An examination of program effects on mediating variables. *Health Education and Behavior* 24, no. 2: 165–76.

Harmon, M. A. 1993. Reducing the risk of drug involvement among early adolescents: An evaluation of Drug Abuse Resistance Education D.A.R.E. *Evaluation Review* 17: 221–39.

Kethmeni, S., D. A. Leamy, and L. Guyon. 1991. *Evaluation of the Drug Abuse Resistance Education Program in Illinois: Preliminary Report.* Urbana-Champaign: Illinois State University.

Kochis, D. S. 1993. *The effectiveness of D.A.R.E: Does it work?* Glassboro, N.J.: Rowan University Law and Justice Department.

McDonald, R. M., D. B. Towberman, and J. L. Hague. 1990. *Volume II: 1989 Impact Assessment of Drug Abuse Resistance Education in the Commonwealth of Virginia.* Richmond: Virginia Commonwealth University, Institute for Research in Justice and Risk Administration.

McMahon, S., and R. J. Wuoreman. 1992. *D.A.R.E. Evaluation for September–January 1991/1992.* Bellevue, Wash.: Bellevue Police Department.

Murray, D. M., and P. J. Hannan. 1990. Planning for the appropriate analysis in school-based drug-use prevention studies. *Journal of Consulting and Clinical Psychology* 58: 458–68.

Nyre, G. F. 1984. *An evaluation of Project D.A.R.E.* Los Angeles, Calif.: Evaluation and Training Institute.

Ralph, N., and C. McMenamy. 1996. Treatment outcomes in an adolescent chemical dependency program. *Adolescence* 31: 91–107.

Silva, R. 1991. *Evaluation of Idaho's D.A.R.E. DNA Abuse Resistance Education Projects*. Meridian: Idaho State Department of Law Enforcement.

Taylor, G. R. 2000. *Integrating quantitative and qualitative research methods*. Lanham, Md.: University Press of America.

———. 2002. *Assessment strategies for individuals with disabilities*. Lewiston, N.Y.: The Edwin Mellen Press.

Weiner, R. L., C. Prichard, et al. 1993. Evaluation of drug-free schools and community program. *Evaluation Review* 17, no. 5: 488–503.

Wiegand, B. 1991. *D.A.R.E.: School Fear 1991 Report*. Washington, D.C.: Department of Defense Dependents Schools.

Wysong, F., R. Aniskiewicz, and R. Wright. 1994. Truth in D.A.R.E. *Social Problems* 41: 448–72.

Zagumny, M. J., and M. K. Thompson. 1997. Does D.A.R.E. work? An Evaluation in Rural Tennessee. *Journal of Alcohol and Drug Education* 42: 32–41.

⑩

AN OBJECTIVE EVALUATION OF DRUG EDUCATION TODAY

A plethora of research indicates that the United States has one of the highest rates of alcohol and drug abuse among industrialized nations of the world (Leone 1991). These statistics have alarmed many segments of society and the schools have been given the leadership role to reduce or eliminate the widespread abuse of drugs among our youths, which remains firmly entrenched

It is evident from research findings reported throughout this text that we have not succeeded in decreasing—much less eliminating—youth substance abuse. The National Center on Addiction and Substance Abuse reported that "each year substance use costs our schools at least $41 billion in truancy, special education, and disruption, teacher turnover, and property damage" (Califano 2001, 1).

According to Finn, Willert, and Marable (2003), it is difficult to obtain accurate estimates on the pervasiveness of in-school substance abuse. They concluded, based upon research findings, that anywhere between 6 percent and 25 percent of U.S. students have been under the influence of alcohol and marijuana at some point during school hours.

Research findings concerning the effects of drugs on school performance have shown that youths who abuse drugs have lower grades in school than abstaining students (Hawkins, Catalano, and Miller 1992; Paulson, Coombs, and Richardson 1990). Other findings have revealed that youths who are influenced by substances are less likely to pay attention, take notes, participate in class discussions, perform well on tests, demonstrate appropriate classroom behaviors, and are more frequently involved in physical fighting than nonusers (Dukarm, Byrd, Auinger, and Weitzman 1996).

The schools appear to be the best agency to provide well-constructed and well-designed drug prevention programs because they have been charged with educating our youths. In order to achieve this important task, the schools need the support of community agencies. Consequently, the schools must collaborate and centralize drug education training in the community.

According to Hansen (1996), Hawkins, Catalano, and Miller (1992), and Beman (1995), there are many factors that contribute to drug abuse. Many are deeply rooted in ethnic and cultural values, peer influence, rebellion against parental authority, emotional instability, curiosity, desires for kicks, frustration, feelings of inferiority, and dissatisfaction with the educational process. The schools must address these issues and more.

Legal and political approaches are but two ways that are used to minimize the growing drug abuse problem. In the education of our youths directed toward prevention of drug use and rehabilitation of drug users preventing initial usage and rehabilitating users are key to breaking the vicious drug cycle. Major research findings have shown many drug education programs to be ineffective in reducing drug usage among youths (Taylor 1972).

Reasons given have been articulated in chapters 1 and 8. Effective drug education programs must be "youth centered," involving youths in all aspects of the program. I have referred to this process as Youths Serving Youths in Drug Education Programs (Y.S.Y.D.E). Specific details concerning this proposed approach are found in chapter 7.

PREVENTION

Kaplin (1996) articulated that prevention needs to involve communities, including families, schools, churches, political, police, media, and the culture, to be effective. There is a preponderance of prevention strategies in chapter 2, and these will only be summarized in this chapter.

Prevention strategies selected for implementation should be based upon the developmental stages of individuals. Drug prevention programs must be collaborative, long term, and involve all segments of the community. A first step would be to define the goals and objectives. Goals and objectives must be realistic and functional for the group served and involve all segments of the community. Refer to appendix G for prevention strategies to employ. Youths should be given facts concerning drugs and be directly involved in developing goals and objectives. Such an approach would make prevention strategies more meaningful to the target group by making methods and procedures more sensitive to them (Dietz 1992; Brown 1997).

Constructing and implementing drug prevention programs involves detailed and systematic planning, which must reflect the traits, characteristics, and cultural values of the group that may affect an individual's decision to use alcohol, tobacco, and drugs. An understanding of racial, ethnic, and community patterns of substance intake and use is essential to functional and realistic substance abuse and prevention programs (Botvin, Schinke, Epstein, and Diaz 1995; Oetting, Donner-Meyer, and Plested 1995; Catalano et al. 1993; Donaldson, Graham, and Hansen 1994).

PARENTAL INVOLVEMENT

Several crucial issues are involved in planning, constructing, implementing, and evaluating drug prevention programs; parental involvement ranks high on the list. Educators need the support and involvement of parents if any drug prevention program is to be successful (Rosenbaum 1998; Szapocnik 1995; National PTA 1996; Domino and Carroll 1994). Parents, as well as all professionals working with drug prevention programs, need in-service training to understand the scope of the many problems that will be presented (Peele 1998; De Miranda 1998; Spoth and Redmond 1995; Bickel 1995; Cohen and Linton 1995).

If properly trained, parents can serve as valuable resources in many aspects of the drug program, such as developing drug curricula, serving as resource individuals, serving as role models, preparing drug literature, and operating audiovisual equipment. At home, parents can monitor the behaviors of their children; in their community, they can serve as neighborhood watchers, and organize and instruct after-school and weekend programs stressing drug prevention.

CURRICULUM DEVELOPMENT

Educators can employ numerous strategies in developing functional drug curricula. Many of these strategies have been articulated in chapters 6, 7, and 9, and include (1) functional assessments, (2) functional curriculum, (3) effective and efficient instructional techniques, (4) comprehensive programs based upon the culture of the community, (5) appropriate staff and resources, and (6) procedural safeguards for protecting student information (Rutherford and Howell 1997; Quinn, Osher, Hoffman, and Hanley 1998; Howell, Fox, and Morehead 1993; Eber 1997; Woodruff et al. 1998).

FUNCTIONAL ASSESSMENT

Assessment of students' needs for the development of educational and treatment plans is essential to successful programs. Functional assessment procedures identify students' strengths and skill deficits that interfere with educational achievement and social/emotional adjustment. This form of assessment is based on identifying students' needs in relation to the curriculum and to their individual needs, rather than on global achievement or ability measures.

Functional assessment is also a continuous process, not static, and results can be used to make systematic adjustments to the student's educational program (Howell, Fox, and Morehead 1993). Assessment procedures should include curriculum-based evaluation and measurement procedures to monitor overall student performance and improvement. To accomplish this assessment, the academic, social skills, and drug curricula for the student must be clarified and implemented.

FUNCTIONAL CURRICULUM

A functional educational curriculum allows the program to meet a student's individual, social, behavioral, and drug prevention needs. In addition to academic skills, a curriculum that focuses on drugs can include developing functional job-related skills, daily living skills, and social skills. Although most alternative education programs do not have comprehensive vocational programs on site, the development of basic work skills tied to job-related social and life skills training is often an important component of a student's individual education plan (IEP). Effective alternative programs sometimes provide the opportunity for part-time employment and access to vocational training in the community.

EFFECTIVE AND EFFICIENT INSTRUCTION

Functional instruction uses positive and direct student-centered instructional strategies that are aligned with functional assessment measures and the curriculum. In this situation, instruction specifically addresses the short-term objectives in the student's IEP that are based on the results of the functional assessment, as well as the standards specified in the general education curriculum. A student's progress toward mastery of these objectives and standards is monitored using ongoing data-collection procedures.

Effective and efficient instruction can also involve the use of social intervention strategies for meaningful intervention in alternative classrooms. Behavioral interventions include a variety of procedures to teach acceptable replacement behaviors, enhance and support appropriate behaviors, and reduce inappropriate behaviors (Hansen, Johnson, Flay, Graham, and Sobel 1998).

COMPREHENSIVE PROGRAMS

Comprehensive programs provide coordinated services to drug-dependent students in alternative settings. Alternative programs can offer a continuum of education and treatment services (e.g., direct instruction, pullout programs, therapeutic programs) to best meet the individual needs of students.

In alternative programs with separate education and treatment facilities, it is important that staff develop common goals and objectives for student success. In addition, coordinated and comprehensive linkages must be developed among the public schools, the alternative education program, the student's family, and social service agencies. Unless agencies collaborate, programs often lead to fragmented services for these youths. Educational, social service, juvenile justice, and mental health agencies must be linked by providing a system of "wraparound" programming (Eber 1997) where coordinated, cooperative, and comprehensive services are implemented to serve students with disabilities. Wraparound programming is a process for developing realistic behavior plans linking the student, the alternative program staff, families, public school personnel, and staff of the different social service agencies (Woodruff et al. 1998).

APPROPRIATE STAFF AND RESOURCES

Drug education programs in alternative settings must provide a full continuum of educational services, including instruction in academics, independent living skills, social skills, work-related skills, and to ensure procedural protections, including parental notification of evaluation and parental involvement in the program. Additionally, effective drug education programs require educators to be sensitive to the needs, interests, parental use of drugs, religion, and ethnic composition of the group. Refer to chapters 3, 4, 5, and 8 for specific information concerning appropriate staff and resources.

In addition to the list of strategies for developing programs in drug education, planners must be aware of the developmental stages of children and youths. These developmental stages largely depend upon the constitution of the curriculum. The following stages are recommended:

1. Stage 1 (ages 5–7): Children should be taught the role of medical drugs in combating illnesses and diseases.
2. Stage 2 (ages 7–10): The harmful effects of commonly used drugs should be explained and exhibited.
3. Stage 3 (ages 11–15): Demonstrations and illustrations should be conducted showing how drug abuse affects the health of the body.
4. Stage 4 (ages 15–18): Expand the concepts concerning the effects of drugs on one's physical, mental, and social conditions.

These stages are recommendations only; school districts should be free to experiment with various stages, as well as to integrate and infuse drug education within the curriculum. The guidelines in chapter 5 are highly recommended in developing drug education programs. School districts should adapt and modify them as needed.

MINORITY YOUTHS

Native Americans, Mexican Americans, Puerto Ricans, and African Americans exhibit a higher prevalence of illicit drug use, heavy cigarette use, alcohol dependence, and need for illicit drug treatment, while Asian/Pacific Islanders, Caribbean Americans, Central Americans, and Cuban Americans have a lower prevalence (Colon 1998; Hernandez 2000; Nofz 1998; U.S. Department of Justice 1993; Mauer and Huling 1995; Grob and DeRios 1992). Regardless of racial/ethnic subgroups, individuals residing in the West or in metropolitan areas with populations greater than one million have a relatively high prevalence of illicit drug use. Characteristics of these individuals include the lack of health insurance, unemployment, no more than nine to eleven years of school, and never having married. Additionally, adolescents who dropped out of school or who reside in households with only one biological parent have a relatively high prevalence of cigarette, alcohol, and illicit drug use (Katims, Zapata, and Yin 1996; U.S. Department of Health and Human Services 2002; Substance Abuse and Mental Services Administration 1998).

INDIVIDUALS WITH DISABILITIES

Individuals with disabilities may be found in all minority groups. Generally, when compared with their peers, disabled individuals have a higher rate of substance abuse. Factors contributing to this high rate of substance abuse include, but are not limited to (1) poor self-image, (2) high frustration rates, (3) peer pressure, and (4) stress factors (Helwing and Holicky 1994; Ogborne and Smart 1995; Hubbard, Everett, and Khan 1996).

Research findings support the notion that individuals with disabilities are more likely to use or abuse alcohol or drugs when compared with their peers (Moore and Polsgrove 1991; Leone 1991; Johnson 1998; Leone, Greenberg, Trickett, and Spero 1989; Genne-Philips 1993; Hubbard, Everett, and Khan 1996). Some groups of disabled individuals—those with emotional, behavioral, hyperactive, and attention problems—appear to have higher rates of drug usage than other individuals classified as disabled (Leone 1991; Flower and Tisdale 1992; Kress and Elias 1993).

Very few programs have been developed to prevent drug usage among individuals with disabilities. There is an urgent need for such programs to be developed. Strategies outlined in chapter 7 can be modified and adapted to meet the unique needs of this population (Moore and Ford 1991; Drug Education 1991).

As early as 1987, the U.S. Department of Education articulated that special educators needed to develop positive alternatives to the punitive responses that characterize many school substance abuse policies in treating drug problems of individuals with disabilities. Unfortunately, in 2002, many schools still employ punitive responses in treating disabled individuals with drug problems (U.S. Department of Education 1987). Educators need to become informed and trained concerning the drug culture in communities; agencies need to treat individuals with drug problems through interagency collaboration within the communities (Johnson 1998; Pentz, Dwyer, MacKinnon, Flay, Hansen, Wang, and Johnson 1989). Because disabled individuals who are drug dependent are not covered under Individuals with Disabilities Education Act (IDEA), they are not entitled to special education and related services (Quinn and Rutherford 1998; Individuals with Disabilities Education Action Amendments PL107-17 1997). In order to provide treatment to disabled individuals who are drug dependent, alternative programs within special education programs have been developed.

The 1997 Amendments to IDEA contain new regulations about sending students to alternative educational settings for drug and weapon violations or "substantial evidence that maintaining the current placement of the child is substantially likely to result in injury to the child or to others" (Section 300.521). As a result, the number of students in alternative drug programs could increase. Therefore, some of the education staff of alternative programs should have special education certification, and support staff should have extensive training in how to serve students with disabilities. Multidisciplinary education and treatment teams also must be established in alternative schools and programs (Quinn and Rutherford 1998).

EVALUATION

In studies completed by Botvin (1986, 1991), data showed that social skills training demonstrated a significant reduction in substance use; percentages showed a reduction from 75 percent to 42 percent. Evaluation of life skills training showed a significant decrease in the use of cigarettes, alcohol, and marijuana by twelve- and thirteen-year-old youths; percentages showed a reduction from 83 percent to 50 percent. Hansen's (1992) research supports the value of psychosocial intervention in reducing substance abuse.

A systematic evaluation design is needed to effectively evaluate the effectiveness of drug education programs on youths (Losciuto 1998). Self-evaluations have proven to be valuable in assessing youths' perceptions relevant to drug prevention programs. Information from all forms of evaluation should be employed to make changes in future drug prevention programs. Refer to chapter 9 for a proposed drug program designed to eliminate or reduce flaws in drug abuse education programs.

Strategies outlined in this text do not require great sums of money to implement. Many of the strategies can be infused and integrated within the curriculum. Most of the expenses will be for resource individuals, materials, and resources. Funds are available through federal funding to assist school districts. (See chapter 7 for funding sources.) Innovative and informed individuals are needed to implement drug programs. Implementing the evaluation model in chapter 9 will provide information on testing and determining the effectiveness of programs. Programs should address the ethnicity, developmental levels, and personalities of youths.

Drug education programs should:

1. Emphasize people, not drugs.
2. Be taught in the schools by teachers, with the collaboration of community agencies.

3. Involve students; they should have a principal part in planning, constructing, and evaluating the programs.
4. Make it clear that drugs are not needed to attain success.
5. Be varied, interdisciplinary, and community-wide.

REFERENCES

Beman, D. S. 1995. Risk factors leading to adolescent substance abuse. *Adolescence* 30:201–208.

Bickel, A. S. 1995. *Family involvement: Strategies for comprehensive alcohol, tobacco, and other drug use prevention programs.* Portland, Ore.: Western Center for Drug-Free Schools and Communities. ED 388 931.

Botvin, G. 1986. Substance abuse prevention research: Recent development and future directions. *Journal of School Health* 56, no. 9:369–74.

———. 1991. *Tobacco, alcohol, and drug abuse prevention through life skills training: Generalizability to multiple populations.* Ithaca, N.Y.: Cornell Medical College, Department of Public Health Report.

Botvin, G. J., S. P. Schinke, J. A. Epstein, T. Diaz, et al. 1995. Effectiveness of culturally focused and generic skills training approaches to alcohol and drug abuse prevention among minority adolescents: Two-year follow-up results. *Psychology of Addictive Behaviors* 9:183–94.

Brown, J. H. 1997. Listen to the kids. *American School Board Journal* 184, no. 12:38–47.

Califano, J. A. 2001. *Malignant neglect: Substance abuse and American's schools.* New York: National Center on Addiction and Substance Abuse at Columbia University.

Catalano, R. F., J. D. Hawkins, C. Krenz, M. Gillmore, D. Morrison, E. Wells, and R. Abbott. 1993. Using research to guide culturally appropriate drug abuse prevention. *Journal of Counseling and Clinical Psychology* 61:804–11.

Cohen, D. A., and K. L. P. Linton. 1995. Parents participation in an adolescent drug abuse prevention program. *Journal of Drug Education* 25, no. 2:159–69.

Colon, E. 1998. Alcohol use among Latino males: Implications for the development of culturally competent prevention and treatment services. In *Alcohol use/abuse among Latinos: Issues and examples of culturally competent services*, edited by M. Delgado. New York: Haworth Press.

De Miranda, J. 1998. What do I tell my son about marijuana? *The Counselor* (May–June).

Dietz, P. M. 1992. Youth-reaching-youth project. *Journal of Emotional and Be-havioral Problems* 1, no. 3:32–34.

Domino, V.A., and K. M. Carroll. 1994. Back to basics: Collaborating the fam-ily school-wide, curriculum-wide. *Schools in the Middle* 4, no. 2 (November): 13–17.

Donaldson, S., J. Graham, and W. Hansen. 1994. Testing the generalizability of intervening mechanisms theories: Understanding the effects of adolescent drug use prevention interventions. *Journal of Behavioral Medicine* 17, no. 2:195–216.

Drug Education Bypasses Most Special Education Students. 1991. In *Educa-tion of the Handicapped* 17, no. 5 (February): 102.

Dukarm, C. P., R. S. Byrd, P. Auinger, and M. Weitzman. 1996. Illicit substance use, gender, and the risk of violent behavior among adolescents. *Archives of Pediatric and Adolescent Medicine* 150:797–801.

Eber, L. 1997. Improving school-based behavioral interventions through use of the wraparound process. *Reaching Today's Youth* 1, no. 2:32–36.

Finn, K. V., H. J. Willert, and M. A. Marable. 2003. Substance use in school. *Educational Leadership* 60, no. 6:80–83.

Flower, R. E., and P. C. Tisdale. 1992. Special education students as a high-risk group for substance abuse: Teachers' perceptions. *School Counselor* 40:103–8.

Genne-Phillips, M. 1993. Treating a special population: The developmentally disabled. *Addict Recovery* 13, no. 6:31–33.

Grob, C., and M. D. DeRios. 1992. Adolescent drug use in cross-cultural per-spective. *The Journal of Drug Issues* 22, no. 1:126–39.

Hansen, W. B. 1992. School-based substance abuse prevention: A review of the state of the art in curriculum, 1980–1990. *Health Education Review* 7, no. 3:403–30.

Hansen, W. B. 1996, September. Prevention programs: What are critical factors that spell success? Paper presented at the National Institute of Drug Abuse National Conference on Drug Abuse Prevention Research, Washington, D.C. At http://165.112.78.61/meetsum/CODA/CODAIndex.html (accessed August 6, 2003).

Hansen, W. B., C. A. Johnson, B. R. Flay, J. W. Graham, and J. L. Sobel. 1998. Affective and social influences approaches to the prevention of multiple sub-stance abuse among seventh grade students: Results from Project SMART. *Preventive Medicine* 17:1–20.

Hawkins, J. D., R. F. Catalano, and J. Y. Miller. 1992. Risk and protective fac-tors for alcohol and other drug problems in adolescence and early adulthood: Implications for substance abuse prevention. *Psychological Bulletin* 112, no. 1:64–105.

Helwing, A. A., and T. Holicky. 1994. Substance abuse in persons with disabilities: Treatment consideration. *Journal of Counseling and Development* 22, no. 3:227–33.

Hernandez, M. 2000. Puerto Rican families and substance abuse. In *Bridges to recovery: Addiction, family therapy, and multicultural treatment*, edited by J. A. Krestan. New York: Free Press.

Howell, K. W., S. S. Fox, and M. K. Morehead. 1993. *Curriculum-based evaluation*. 2nd ed. Belmont, Calif.: Brooks/Cole.

Hubbard, J. R., A. S. Everett, and M. A. Khan. 1996. Alcohol and drug abuse in patients with physical disabilities. *American Journal of Drug and Alcohol Abuse* 22, no. 2 (May): 215–31.

Individuals with Disabilities Education Act Amendments. 1997. *Children, youth, and families*. Washington, D.C.: U.S Government Printing Office.

Johnson, J. L. 1998. The challenge of substance abuse. *Teaching Exceptional Children* 20, no. 4:29–31.

Kaplin, S. 1996. Drug prevention with young people: Defining the model and evaluating effects. *Journal of the Institute of Health Education* 34, no. 4.

Katims, D. S., J. T. Zapata, and Z. Yin. 1996. Risk factors for substance use by Mexican American youth with and without learning disabilities. *Journal of Learning Disabilities* 29:213–19.

Kress, J. S., and M. J. Elias. 1993. Substance abuse prevention in special education populations: Review and recommendations. *Journal of Special Education* 27:35–51.

Leone, P. E. 1991. *Alcohol and other drugs: Use, abuse, and disabilities*. Reston, Va.: Council for Exceptional Children.

Leone, P. E., J. M. Greenberg, E. J. Trickett, and E. Spero. 1989. A study of the use of cigarettes, alcohol, and marijuana by students identified as "seriously emotionally disturbed." *Counterpoint* 9, no. 3:6–7.

Losciuto, L. 1998. Evaluation of a drug abuse prevention program: A field experiment. *Addictive Behaviors* 13:337–51.

Mauer, M., and T. Huling. 1995. Young black Americans and the criminal justice system: Five years later. *The Sentencing Project*. Washington, D.C.: U.S. Department of Justice.

Moore, D., and J. A. Ford. 1991. Prevention of substance abuse among persons with disabilities: A demonstration model. *Prevention Forum* 11, no. 2:1–3, 7–10.

Moore, D., and L. Polsgrove. 1991. Disabilities, developmental handicaps, and substance misuse: A review. *The International Journal of Addictions* 26: 65–90.

National PTA. 1996. *Keeping youth drug-free: A guide for parents, grandparents, elders, mentors, and other caregivers*. Chicago, Ill.: National PTA. ED 398 523.

Nofz, M. P. 1988. Alcohol abuse and culturally marginal American Indians. *Social Casework* 69, no. 2:67–73.

Oetting, E. R., J. F. Donner-Meyer, B. A. Plested, et al. 1995. Assessing community readiness for prevention. *International Journal of the Addictions* 30, no. 6:659–83.

Ogborne, A. C., and R. G. Smart. 1995. People with physical disabilities admitted to a residential addiction treatment program. *American Journal of Drug and Alcohol Abuse* 21, no. 1:137–45.

Paulson, M. J., R. H. Coombs, and M. A. Richardson. 1990. School performance, academic aspirations, and drug use among children and adolescents. *Journal of Drug Education* 20:289–303.

Peele, S. 1998. *Don't panic! A parent's guide to understanding and preventing alcohol and drug abuse*. New York: Lindesmith Center.

Pentz, M. A., J. H. Dwyer, D. P. MacKinnon, B. R. Flay, W. B. Hansen, E. U. I. Wang, and C. A. Johnson. 1989. A multi-community trial for primary prevention of adolescent drug abuse. *Journal of the American Medical Association* 261, no. 22:3259–66.

Quinn, M. M., D. Osher, C. C. Hoffman, and T. V. Hanley. 1998. *Safe, drug-free, and effective schools for all students: What works*. Washington, D.C.: American Institutes for Research.

Quinn, M. M., and R. B. Rutherford. 1998. *Alternative programs for students with social, emotional, and behavioral problems*. Reston, Va.: Council for Exceptional Children.

Rosenbaum, M. 1998. A mother's advice about drugs. *San Francisco Chronicle*, September 7.

Rutherford, R. B., and K. W. Howell. 1997. *Education program assessment: MacLaren Children's Center School*. Los Angeles: Los Angeles County Department of Child and Family Services.

Spoth, R., and C. Redmond. 1995. Parent motivation to enroll in parenting skills programs: A model of family context and health belief predictors. *Journal of Family Psychology* 9, no. 3:294–310.

Substance Abuse and Mental Health Services Administration. 1998. *Prevalence of substance use among racial and ethnic subgroups in the United States, 1991–1993*. Washington, D.C.: U.S. Government Printing Office.

Szapocnik, K. J., ed. 1995. *A Hispanic/Latino family approach to substance abuse prevention*. CSAP Cultural Competence Series 2. Rockville, Md.: Center for Substance Abuse Prevention. ED 400 489.

Taylor, G. R. 1972. Toward a model K–12 program in drug education. *Thrust for Education Leadership* 1, no. 4:28–32.

U.S. Department of Education. 1987. *District effects in substance abuse education*. Washington, D.C.: Office of Educational Research and Improvement.

U.S. Department of Health and Human Services. 2002. At www.Samhsa.gov/oas/NHSDA/Ethnic/eth H1006.htm.   ·

U.S. Department of Justice, Bureau of Justice Statistics. 1993. *Sentencing in the federal courts: Does race matter? The transition to sentencing guidelines, 1986–1990.* Washington, D.C.: U.S. Government Printing Office.

Woodruff, D., D. Osher, C. C. Hoffman, A., Gruner, M. A. King, S. T. Snow, and J. C. McIntire. 1998. *The role of education in a system of care: Effectively serving children with emotional or behavioral disorders. Systems of Care. Promising Practices in Children's Mental Health.* Vol. 3. Washington, D.C.: Center for Effective Collaboration and Practice, American Institute for Research.

Appendix A

IMPROVING AMERICA'S SCHOOLS ACT

SECTION 4116. LOCAL DRUG AND VIOLENCE PREVENTION PROGRAMS

(a) Program Requirements. A local educational agency shall use funds received under this subpart to adopt and carry out a comprehensive drug and violence prevention program which shall
   (1) be designed, for all students and employees, to prevent the use, possession, and distribution of tobacco, alcohol, and illegal drugs by students and to prevent the illegal use, possession, and distribution of such substances by employees;
   (2) include activities to promote the involvement of parents and coordination with community groups and agencies, including the distribution of information about the local educational agency's needs, goals, and programs under this subpart.
(b) Authorized Activities. A comprehensive drug and violence prevention program carried out under this subpart may include
   (1) age-appropriate, developmentally based drug prevention and education programs for all students, from the preschool level through grade 12, that address the legal, social, personal and health consequences of the use of illegal drugs, promote a sense of individual responsibility, and provide information about effective techniques for resisting peer pressure to use illegal drugs;

(2)　programs of drug prevention, comprehensive health education, early intervention, pupil services, mentoring, or rehabilitation referral, which emphasize students' sense of individual responsibility and which may include

(A)　the dissemination of information about drug prevention;

(B)　the professional development of school personnel, parents, students, law enforcement officials, judicial officials, health service providers and community leaders in prevention, education, early intervention, pupil services or rehabilitation referral; and

(C)　the implementation of strategies to integrate the delivery of services from a variety of providers, to combat illegal alcohol, tobacco and drug use, such as—

(i)　family counseling;

(ii)　early intervention activities that prevent family dysfunction, enhance school performance, and boost attachment to school and family; and

(iii)　activities, such as community service and service-learning projects, that are designed to increase students' sense of community;

(3)　age-appropriate, developmentally based violence prevention and education programs for all students, from the preschool level through grade 12, that address the legal, health, personal, and social consequences of violent and disruptive behavior, including sexual harassment and abuse, and victimization associated with prejudice and intolerance, and that include activities designed to help students develop a sense of individual responsibility and respect for the rights of others, and to resolve conflicts without violence;

(4)　violence prevention programs for school-aged youth, which emphasize students' sense of individual responsibility and may include

(A)　the dissemination of information about school safety and discipline;

(B)　the professional development of school personnel, parents, students, law enforcement officials, judicial officials, and community leaders in designing and implementing strategies to prevent school violence;

(C)　the implementation of strategies, such as conflict resolution and peer mediation, student outreach efforts against violence, anti-crime youth councils (which work with school and community-based organizations to discuss and develop crime prevention strategies), and the use of mentoring programs, to combat school violence and other forms of disruptive behavior, such as sexual harassment and abuse; and

(D) the development and implementation of character education programs, as a component of a comprehensive drug or violence prevention program, that are tailored by communities, parents and schools; and

(E) comprehensive, community-wide strategies to prevent or reduce illegal gang activities;

(5) supporting "safe zones of passage" for students between home and school through such measures as Drug- and Weapon-Free School Zones, enhanced law enforcement, and neighborhood patrols;

(6) acquiring and installing metal detectors and hiring security

(7) personnel; awareness of and sensitivity to alternatives to violence through courses of study that include related issues of intolerance and hatred in history;

(8) the promotion of before- and after-school recreational, instructional, cultural, and artistic programs in supervised community settings;

(9) drug abuse resistance education programs, designed to teach students to recognize and resist pressures to use alcohol or other drugs, which may include activities such as classroom instruction by uniformed law enforcement officers, resistance techniques, resistance to peer pressure and gang pressure, and provision for parental involvement; and

(10) the evaluation of any of the activities authorized under this subsection.

Limitations

(1) In general. Not more than 20 percent of the funds made available to a local educational agency under this subpart may be used to carry out the activities described in paragraphs (5) and (6) of subsection (b).

(2) Special rule. A local educational agency shall only be able to use funds received under this subpart for activities described

in paragraphs (5) and (6) of subsection (b) if funding for such activities is not received from other Federal agencies.

(3)   Administrative Provisions. Notwithstanding any other provisions of law, any funds expended prior to July 1, 1995, under part B of the Drug-Free Schools and Communities Act of 1986 (as in effect prior to enactment of the Improving America's Schools Act) for the support of a comprehensive school health program shall be deemed to have been authorized by part B of such Act.

Appendix B

ERIC DIGEST: ERIC CLEARINGHOUSE ON INFORMATION AND TECHNOLOGY

LIBRARIES FOR THE NATIONAL EDUCATION GOALS

By the year 2000, it is envisioned that our nation will have accomplished the six National Education Goals adopted in 1990 by the President and the governors of the United States. Since libraries are the only educational system available to everyone, regardless of age or affiliation, it is logical to turn to our nation's libraries to help to achieve these goals.

To demonstrate the critical role libraries can and do play in support of the national education initiatives, an extensive literature review and analysis was undertaken (Stripling, 1992). This digest highlights the findings of that review.

GOAL ONE: By the Year 2000, All Children in American Will Start School Ready to Learn

Experts predict that 50 percent of a child's intellectual development occurs before the age of four. If this is true, then it is crucial that preschoolers receive high-quality care. Both public and school libraries provide activities, services, and materials to facilitate early language acquisition and reading readiness in preschool children.

Highlights:

- The Pittsburgh Public Library's Beginning with Books project reached disadvantaged families in places around the community. They began by distributing packets to preschoolers in health clinic waiting rooms, and later expanded to social services centers, shelters, housing developments, and day care centers.
- The Foster Reading Center was set up by the Evanston (Illinois) Public Library and community leaders to provide reading/learning centers in the neighborhoods. Its Roving Reader Project sends readers to day care centers twice a week to share stories and enthusiasm for reading.

GOAL TWO: By the Year 2000, the High School Graduation Rate Will Increase to At Least 90 Percent

School and public libraries are joining together to offer special programs for students who are most at risk of dropping out before graduation. In addition to literacy programs, libraries are offering programs that address self-esteem and ethnic pride, motivation, thinking and study skills, and the development of interests.

Highlights:

- The Reuben McMillan Free Library Association (Youngstown, Ohio) conducts programs on ethnic heritage for at-risk and minority students. Programs have featured African-American writers, Hispanic crafts, and other topics. Students continue to visit the library after attending special programs.
- The Rantoul (Illinois) Public Library's at-risk program offers volunteer tutoring during students' study halls, educational seminars and workshops, field trips to businesses, and pre-employment experiences at local businesses.

**GOAL THREE: By the Year 2000, American Students Will Leave
Grades 4, 8, and 12 Having Demonstrated Competency in
Challenging Subject Matter Including English, Mathematics, Science,
History, and Geography; and Every School in America Will Ensure
That All Students Learn to Use Their Minds Well, So They May Be
Prepared for Responsible Citizenship, Further Learning, and
Productive Employment in Our Modern Economy**

With the quantity of information doubling every few years, students
cannot be expected to memorize all the facts about a given subject. Instead, students must develop their ability to think and to learn independently. School libraries can be instrumental in teaching students how to
find and process information using technology as a tool. By providing
equitable access to information, libraries can help students to make responsible decisions and to become productive citizens.

Highlights:

- Research shows that students perform better on tests of research
  skills and comprehension skills when they have access to a good library media center and a professional library media specialist.
- In Hinsdale, Illinois, school and public libraries jointly published a
  student literary magazine. The program resulted in increased student self-confidence, improved reading skills, more creative and
  better organized thinking, and greater ability to express thoughts
  and feelings through writing.

**GOAL FOUR: By the Year 2000, U.S. Students Will Be the First in
the World in Science and Mathematics Achievement**

Libraries play a unique role in bridging the gaps between disciplines, and,
more specifically, in helping students apply science and mathematics concepts to other disciplines. Science curricula can be enriched in library media centers by providing hands-on displays and learning centers, electronic
databases that contain the latest scientific information, guest speakers and
demonstrations, and displays of student-produced science projects.

Highlights:

- The Monroe County Public Library (Stroudsburg, Pennsylvania) has a science awareness program for children. Volunteers demonstrate natural and scientific phenomena at special presentations, and resources in science and technology are distributed to teachers. Students use the school library media center to access electronic bulletin boards and databases available on national networks. NASA Spacelink, for example, provides current information and teaching guides on topics about space.

GOAL FIVE: By the Year 2000, Every Adult American Will Be Literate and Will Possess the Knowledge and Skills Necessary to Compete in a Global Economy and Exercise the Rights and Responsibilities of Citizenship

It is estimated that there are 23 million illiterate and 35 million semiliterate adults in America. Many of these people are removed from an established educational system, and for these people, the library is the only educational institution available. Libraries are responding by providing services and materials to help American citizens gain literacy and become lifelong learners. Library literacy programs frequently target such special audiences as young adults, disabled people, institutionalized people, and people with limited English proficiency.
Highlights:

- The Brooklyn Public Library operates five adult learning centers that feature tutoring and tutor training; computer-assisted learning; English as a Second Language classes; collections of high-interest, low-vocabulary books; reference books for literacy professionals; and study tables on citizenship, job-seeking, and other adult interest.
- The Colorado Alliance of Research Libraries (CARL) online catalog system is located in many libraries and is also accessible to learners at home and schools by modem. In addition to library holdings, the system gives access to economic information, local databases, other computer networks, and electronic mail.

GOAL SIX: By the Year 2000, Every School in America Will Be Free of Drugs and Violence and Will Offer a Disciplined Environment Conducive to Learning

Before learning can take place, students must feel intellectually, physically, and emotionally safe. Libraries provide intellectual and emotional safety for children by offering information and services that children can turn to when seeking answers to their concerns.

Highlights:

- The Geauga West Branch of the Geauga County Public Library (Chesterland, Ohio) has a latchkey program that provides youth programming and help with school assignments while functioning as a safe social interaction center.
- Project LEAD (Librarians and Educators Against Drugs) of the Summit (Illinois) Public Library promotes drug awareness among elementary students by hosting a community awareness day, distributing information, and arranging visits by anti-drug speakers to the schools.

Bibliography

Information 2000: Library and Information Services for the 21st Century. Summary Report of the 1991 White House Conference on Library and Information Services. (1991). Washington, DC: White House Conference on Library and Information Services. ED 341 399.

National Goals for Education. (1990). Washington, DC: Executive Office of the President. ED 319 143.

Public Libraries: Places Where Learning Can Happen. A Report on Selected Programs Supporting the National Education Goals Funded Under the Library Services and Construction Act, Title I. (1992).

Washington, DC: Office of Educational Research and Improvement, Office of Library Programs. IR 254 034. ED number pending. Stripling, Barbara K. (1992). Libraries for the National Education Goals. Syracuse, NY: ERIC Clearinghouse on Information Resources, IR 054 132.ED 345 752.

References identified with an ED (ERIC document) or EJ (ERIC journal) number are cited in the ERIC database. Most documents are available in

ERIC microfiche collections at more than 900 locations worldwide, and can be ordered through EDRS: (800) 443-ERIC. Journal articles are available from the original journal, interlibrary loan services, or article reproduction clearinghouses, such as: UMI (800) 732-0616; or ISI (800) 523-1850. This digest was prepared for the ERIC Clearinghouse on Information and Technology by Mary Alice Brennan, Library Media Specialist, Oxford Academy, Oxford, New York, June 1992. ERIC Digest articles are in the public domain and may be freely reproduced and disseminated. This publication was prepared with funding from the Office of Educational Research and Improvement, U.S. Department of Education, under contract no. R188062008. The opinions expressed in this report do not necessarily reflect the positions of IERI or ED.

ABOUT ERIC DIGEST

ERIC Digests are short reports on topics of current interest in education. Digests are targeted to teachers, administrators, parents, policymakers, and other practitioners. They are designed to provide an overview of information on a given topic with references to items that provide more detailed information. Reviewed by subject experts who are content specialists in the field, the digests are funded by the Office of Educational Research and Improvement (OERI) of the U.S. Department of Education.

Mary Alice Brennan
June 1992

Appendix C

RESOURCES ON
PARENTAL INVOLVEMENT

Appleseed. This nonprofit, national campaign advocates improvement in public schools by increasing parental involvement in U.S. schools. (projectAppleseed.org)

Early Childhood Digest. This quarterly report contains articles about ways schools and families can work together to help children learn. (trnutreg@dqs.dqsys.com)

The National PTA. This site provides a number of documents offering ideas for teachers and schools who want to encourage and promote parental involvement in education. (330 N. Wabash Avenue, Suite 2100, Chicago, IL 60611; phone (312) 670-6782)

National Network of Partnership Schools. Established by researchers at Johns Hopkins University, this organization helps schools, districts, and states develop and maintain programs that promote school-family-community partnerships. (3003 N. Charles Street, Suite 200, Baltimore, MD 21218)

A Pocket Guide to Building Partnerships for Student Learning. The NEA offers suggestions for ways in which both parents and teachers can contribute to effective partnerships. (1201 16th Street, NW, Washington, DC 20036)

Parental Involvement. *Education Week* provides a number of articles about parental involvement in schools.

Appendix D

CURRICULUM RESOURCES

A Guide to School-Based Drug and Alcohol Abuse Prevention Curricula. Health Promotion Research Center, Stanford Center for Research in Disease Prevention, 1000 Welch Road, Palo Alto, CA 94304-1855; (415) 723-1000.

Austin Independent School District. 1989. Taking Steps Towards Drug-Free Schools in AISD. ED 313 494.

Dade County Public Schools. 1989. A Community Education Approach to Substance Abuse. ED 311 341.

Drug Prevention Curricula: A Guide to Selection and Implementation. National Clearinghouse for Alcohol and Drug Information, P.O. Box 2345, Rockville, MD 20852; (301) 468-2600.

National School Safety Center. 1988. Drug Traffic and Abuse in Schools: NSSC Resource Paper. ED 307 530.

U.S. Department of Education. 1990. Learning to Live Drug Free: A Curriculum Model for Prevention. National Clearinghouse for Alcohol and Drug Information, P. O. Box 2345, Rockville, MD 20852; (301) 468-2600.

Appendix E

REFERENCES

Bauman, I. C. 1985. *A Study of Cigarette Smoking Behavior among Youth.* Chapel Hill: Department of Maternal and Child Health, School of Public Health, University of North Carolina. Adolescent Questionnaire.

Becker, H. R., M. E. Agopian, and L. R. Rohach. 1989. Impact Evaluation of Drug Abuse Resistance Education (D.A.R.E.). *Journal of Drug Education* 22: 283–91.

Carstens, S. J., D. J. Pecchia, and L. R. Rohach. 1989. *D.A.R.E.-Drug Abuse Resistance: Is It Jerking?* Minnesota: Robinsdale Area Schools, Independent School District, 281.

Clayton, R. R. 1987. Project D.A.R.E. in Lexington: Evaluation of the Pilot Phase. Unpublished Report. University of Kentucky, Department of Sociology.

Etheridge, B., and S. L. Hicks. 1989. An Evaluation of the North Carolina D.A.R.E. Program. Unpublished Report.

Goode, E., ed. 1991. *Annual Editions: Drugs, Society, and Behavior 91/92.* Guilford, Conn.: Duskin Publishing.

Goodstadt, M. S. 1986. School-based Drug Education in North America: What Is Wrong? What Can Be Done? *Journal of School Health* 56, no. 7: 278–81. EJ 314 990.

McCormick, F. C., and E. R. McCormick. 1992. *An Evaluation of the Third-Year Drug Abuse Resistance Education (D.A.R.E.) Program at St. Paul.* Saint Paul, Minn.: Educational Concepts.

Milgram, G. G. 1987. Alcohol and Drug Education Programs. *Journal of Drug Education* 17: 43–57.

National Commission on Drug-Free Schools. 1990. *Toward a Drug-free Generation: A Nation's Responsibility*. Washington, D.C.: U.S. Department of Education.

Tricker, R., and L. G. Davis. 1988. Implementing Drug Education in Schools: An Analysis of Costs and Teacher Perceptions. *Journal of School Health* 58, no. 5: 181–85. EJ 378 228.

U.S. Department of Education. 1990. *National Goals for Education*. Washington, D.C.: U. S. Department of Education.

Note: References identified with an EJ or ED number have been abstracted and are in the ERIC database. Journal articles (EJ) should be available at most research libraries; documents (ED) are available in ERIC microfiche collections at more than 700 locations. Documents can also be ordered through the ERIC Document Reproduction Service: (800) 443-3742. For more information, contact the ERIC Clearinghouse on Teacher Education, One Dupont Circle NW, Suite 610, Washington, DC 20036-2412; (202) 293-2450.

Appendix F

PROGRAM EVALUATION RESOURCES

Understanding Evaluation: The Way to Better Prevention Programs provides introductory information about evaluating drug prevention programs. This publication is available from the Safe and Drug-Free Schools Program, Education Public Center, U.S. Department of Education at 1-877-433-7827.

Prevention Plus III: Assessing Alcohol and Other Drug Prevention Programs at the School and Community Level. A four-step guide to useful program assessment publish by Office of Substance Abuse Programs provides program evaluation worksheets tailored to meet the needs of school and community personnel who want to assess their own program. Available from the National Clearinghouse for Alcohol and Drug Information at (800) 729-6686.

Helping Communities Fight Crime: Comprehensive Planning Techniques, Model Programs, and Resources provides a catalog to help communities find and use the tools they need to develop, implement, and sustain effective crime and violence prevention effort. This publication and other information are from the National Criminal Justice Reference Service at (800) 851-3428.

Preventing Drug Use among Children and Adolescents: A Research-Based Guide, published by NIDA, is designed to provide important research-based concepts and information to further efforts to develop and carry out effective drug abuse prevention programs. Available from the National Clearinghouse for Alcohol and Drug Information (800) 729-6686.

Safe and Drug-Free Schools

U.S. Department of Education

http://www.ed.gov/offices/OESE/SDFS

This site provides focuses on drug and violence prevention activities at the
U.S. Department of Education, including information on upcoming activities, budget, updates, and grant opportunities.

National Institutes of Health

Gopher:// gopher.nih.gov

http://www.nih.gov

U.S. Department of Health and Human Services

Gopher://gopher.os.dhhs.gov

www.os.dhhs.gov

Asian American Resources

www.ncadi.samsha.gov/govstudy/shortreports/language.txl

Alcoholics Anonymous Information and Literature

http://www.moscow.com:80/Resources/SelfHelp/AA/./

The Center for Substance Abuse Research (CESAR at the University of Maryland College Park)

http://www.cesar.umd.edu/

Hmong Homepage

http://www.stolaf.edu/people/cdr/hmong/

Japanese Information

www.ncadi.samsha.gov/govstudy/shortreports/language.txl

Korea Network Information Center

www.ncadi.samsha.gov/govstudy/shortreports/language.tx

Men's Issues Page

http://www.vix.com/men

SafetyNet: Domestic Violence Resources

http://www.interport.net/~asherman/dv.html

World Health Organization (WHO)

http://www.who.ch

Appendix G

PREVENTION PRINCIPLES FOR CHILDREN AND ADOLESCENTS

Prevention programs should be designed to enhance "protective factors" and move toward reversing or reducing known "risk factors."

Prevention programs should target all forms of drug abuse, including the use of tobacco, alcohol, marijuana, and inhalants.

Prevention programs should include skills to resist drugs when offered, strengthen personal commitments against drug use, and increase social competency (e.g., in communications, peer relationships, self-efficacy, and assertiveness), in conjunction with reinforcement of attitudes against drug use.

Prevention programs for adolescents should include interactive methods, such as peer discussion groups, rather than didactic teaching techniques alone.

Prevention programs should include a parents' or caregivers' component that reinforces what the children are learning (such as facts about drugs and their harmful effects) and that opens opportunities for family discussions about use of legal and illegal substances and family policies about their use.

Prevention programs should be long term (over the entire school career) with repeat interventions to reinforce the original prevention goals. For example, school-based efforts directed at elementary and middle school students should include booster sessions to help with critical transitions from middle to high school.

Family-focused prevention efforts have a greater impact than strategies that focus on parents only or children only.

Community programs that include media campaigns and policy changes, such as new regulations that restrict access to alcohol, tobacco, or other drugs, are more effective when they are accompanied by school and family interventions.

Community programs need to strengthen norms against drug use in all drug abuse prevention settings, including the family, the school, and the community.

Schools should offer opportunities to reach all populations and also serve as important settings for specific subpopulations at risk for drug abuse, such as children with behavior problems or learning disabilities and those who are potential dropouts.

Prevention programming should be adapted to address the specific nature of the drug abuse problem in the local community.

The higher the level of risk of the target population, the more intensive the prevention effort must be and the earlier it must begin.

Prevention programs should be age specific, developmentally appropriate, and culturally sensitive.

Effective prevention programs are cost effective. For every dollar spent on drug use prevention, communities can save $4 to $5 in costs for drug abuse treatment and counseling.

GLOSSARY

Abuse   Taking a drug for other than that prescribed.

Addiction   Characterized by the compulsive use of a substance resulting in physical or psychological dependency. Is usually accompanied by increased tolerance.

Amphetamines   *Speed, Uppers, Pep Pills, Dexedrine, Bumblebees.* Capsules, pills, or tablets injected, inhaled, or taken orally. Headaches, blurred vision, dizziness, fatigue, irregular heart beat, loss of coordination, and hallucinations.

Barbiturates   *Downers, Barbs, Blue Devils, Yellow Jacket, Red Devils.* Yellow, blue, or red and blue capsules taken orally. Similar to alcohol, calmness, slurred speech, staggering, altered perception, violent temper.

Cocaine   *Coke, Snow, Flake, White, Blow.* White crystalline powder inhaled, injected, smoked. Dilated pupils, elevated blood pressure, and damage to the nervous system.

Crack   *Freebase Rocks, Rock.* Light brown or white pellets or crystalline rocks that look like soap. Smoked same as above. Hallucinations, paranoia, seizures, and cardiac arrest.

Drugs of Abuse   Substances taken in any way to alter mood, perception, or brain function. From prescribed drugs to alcohol to solvents.

Experimental   Use implies trying a drug only once or twice.

Habituation   Is the result of continued casual use and can be characterized as the need to take a drug at given times to avoid the anxiety associated with not taking it.

Heroin   *Junk, Smack, Horse, Brown Sugar, Big H, Black Tar.* Powder, white to dark brown tarlike substance. Injected, inhaled, smoked. Drowsiness, nausea, shallow breathing, clammy skin, and convulsions.

Lysergic Acid Diethylamide   *LSD, Acid, Green Dragon, White Lightning, Blue Heaven, Sugar Cubes.* Bright-colored tablets, blotter paper, thin squares of gelatin, clear liquid. Taken orally, licked off paper; gelatin and liquid can be put into the eyes. Illusion, hallucinations, dilated pupils, and increased heart rate.

Marijuana   *Pot, Grass, Weed, Dried Parsley.* Eaten or smoked. Reduces short-term memory, alters sense of time, lack of coordination.

Mis-use   Taking a drug for its prescribed purpose but not in the way it is supposed to be taken.

Nitrous Oxide   *Laughing Gas, Whippets.* Propellant for whipped cream in aerosol spray can. Vapors inhaled causes headaches, violent behavior, and damage to the nervous system.

Pharmacokinetics   How a substance enters and moves through the body.

Psilocybin   *Mushroom.* Hard brown discs, tablets, capsules, fresh or dried mushrooms, chewed or swallowed. Flashback, panic, anxiety, and loss of control.

Physical Dependency   Is reached when the body has adapted to a drug and cannot function normally without it.

Psychological Dependency   Is an emotional state of craving a drug either for its positive effects or to avoid the negative effects caused by its absence.

Tolerance   Adaptation, which is the body/brain's attempt to establish homeostatis in the presence of a substance.

Tranquilizers   *Valium, Librium, Miltown, Tranxene.* Tablets or capsules taken orally. Fatigue, dizziness.

AUTHOR INDEX

SUBJECT INDEX

African Americans: factors, 106; incidence, 106–107; intervention, 106–107

Asian/Pacific Islanders: factors, 110; incidence, 109–110; intervention, 110

awareness day, 42

changing drug abuse habits, 73–75

children with disabilities: characteristics, 111; classified, 110; factors 110–111; intervention, 111

collaborative efforts, 33, 55–56

communication skills of parents, 54–55

components of a drug program, 79

curriculum development: purpose, 91–92; sequence, 97–98. *Also see* construction, 93–95

curriculum format, 98–99, 138

D.A.R.E. *See* Drug Abuse Resistance Education Program.

developing a comprehensive drug program, 2, 3

developing comprehensive programs, 139–140

developing functional drug education programs: current programs, 78; early intervention, 77; expense of developing, 78; realistic guidelines, 77–78, 79–87; role of the school, 136. *Also see* supporting drug programs.

disability and drug usage, 4, 10–12

drug abuse resistance education program, 5, 41–42

drug intervention strategies: behavior contracting, 23; cognitive behavior, 10, 24, 72–73; contingency contracting, 24; group counseling, 26–27; motivation, 22,

ABOUT THE AUTHOR

George R. Taylor is professor of special education and former chairperson of the Department of Special Education at Coppin State College, and CORE Faculty, The Union Institute and University. His knowledge and expertise in the areas of research and special education are both locally and nationally renown. He has made significant contributions through research and publications in the areas of special education, research, and education. Additionally, Dr. Taylor has directed several large federal research grants and conducted numerous workshops and seminars throughout the country. He is the author of *Informal Classroom Assessment Strategies for Teachers*, and *Using Human Learning Strategies in the Classroom*, and co-author of *Educating the Disabled*, all published by ScarecrowEducation.